The night wind slipped over Sundance Ranch, and from the corral, Robin could hear a horse neigh. How she loved it here, but she had to leave. And she must tell Craig that.

A shaft of moonlight filtered over her face as she turned to him. He was looking into her eyes and shaking his head.

"You just don't understand," he said.

"You're right. I don't understand you at all. How can you be so kind one minute and so gruff and uncaring the next?"

"I don't mean to be gruff." His voice was as soft as the breeze caressing her face. He suddenly seemed so different from the man she had argued with that afternoon. "And I'm certainly not uncaring…"

His head dipped down to kiss her lips, and Robin felt herself torn with frustration and uncertainty. Who was Craig Cameron? She wasn't sure. And yet she was very sure of this: she was falling in love with him, and she couldn't seem to stop herself.

Palisades.
Pure Romance.

A PALISADES CONTEMPORARY ROMANCE

SUNDANCE

PEGGY DARTY

PALISADES

SUNDANCE
published by Palisades
a part of the Questar publishing family

© 1996 by Peggy Darty
International Standard Book Number: 0-88070-952-9

Cover illustration by George Angelini
Cover designed by David Carlson and
Mona Weir-Daly
Edited by Paul Hawley

Printed in the United States of America

For information:
QUESTAR PUBLISHERS, INC.
POST OFFICE BOX 1720
SISTERS, OREGON 97759

96 97 98 99 00 01 02 03 — 10 9 8 7 6 5 4 3 2 1

To Pat and Curtis,
who first told us about beautiful British Columbia.
Thanks for all the good times.
And for Landon, who took me there as a bride.
I'll never forget that wonderful year.

For the LORD God is a sun and shield: the LORD will give grace and glory: no good thing will he withhold from them that walk uprightly.

PSALMS 84:11 (KJV)

One

~~~

W hat a beautiful place," Robin Grayson said to herself as she peered through the windshield of her blue Toyota compact.

The Rockies towered to the east, and the Purcell Mountain Range sprawled across the west side of the valley. Nestled somewhere in between, in its own hidden valley, was the ranch she had heard about all her life: Sundance.

She couldn't wait to see it, but first there was some business to get out of the way. Her foot pressed harder on the accelerator, and without warning a sharp curve loomed before her.

She took the curve wide; too wide, in fact. Her slick tires lost their grip and began to spin. Suddenly she was heading straight for the loose gravel on the side of the highway.

"God help me!" she cried out as the canyon wall loomed toward her, growing closer and closer, while the car fishtailed and skidded sideways into a deep ditch. She sat for a minute, waiting for something to crash and fall apart. Then she began to realize the only thing coming apart was Robin Grayson.

Trembling from head to toe, she leaned back against the seat and took a deep breath. Then she turned her neck, right to left, and flexed her body. Other than feeling the jolt, she had not suffered any real injury.

She reached over to push her creaking door open and crawled out of the car to survey the damage. To her amazement, all she saw on first inspection was a dent on the back fender. It was an absolute miracle, and she should be grateful. But at the moment all she felt was frustration.

"Robin, how could you be so stupid?" she muttered to herself as she climbed the dusty bank to the road. A couple zipped by in a sports car, with eyes only for one another.

She checked her watch. It was one o'clock, and she was thirty minutes late to meet her new employer at the Caribou Café. The fact that she was running late had made her careless, and now she was really in a bind.

Robin swept her hands up the sides of her rumpled jeans and frowned down at her white T-shirt. In assessing the damage to her fender, she had ended up with a layer of dust on her shirt. She ran a hand through her shoulder-length red hair. Her normal style was a layer of waves around her face, but now her hair felt gritty and spiked. She tried to smooth it down, wondering what sort of impression she would make on her new employer. If he was still waiting.

An older model Escort station wagon was traveling east, probably headed to Fort Steele, and she began to wave it down. The vehicle slowed and stopped, but Robin's hopes sank as she saw the passengers: a frail, elderly couple peering at her curiously.

"You hurt, young lady?" the little man called as he got out of the car.

"No, I just need to get my car out of the ditch," she said, glancing back at his small car and doubting that he was the man for the job.

He scratched his white head thoughtfully as he ambled toward her car.

"Don't believe you got much damage," he said, squinting into the ditch. "But you'll need a tow truck or someone with a four-wheel drive." He turned back to face her, his eyes sweeping over her. "Plenty of trucks pass up and down this highway. Pretty girl like you shouldn't have any trouble getting help."

"Thanks. I'm sure someone will stop."

"I reckon so, but you be careful, young lady," he added, shuffling back to his car and opening the door. She could hear a buzz of conversation between him and his wife, probably something to do with how fast young people drive nowadays.

Robin paced the road again, watching, waiting, pondering her bad luck.

She had stopped at her cousin's apartment in Cranbrook last night. Her cousin Kathy Spencer was a small, vivacious brunette who seemed a startling contrast to her father. Doug Spencer looked as though he lived in business suits and found it difficult to loosen up and have a good time. His tall, lean appearance suggested discipline in everything from food to posture. He had made Robin slightly uncomfortable.

Kathy, on the other hand, seemed a bit of a scatterbrain to be a bank teller. Still, Robin liked her immensely. Both were in their mid-twenties, and yet they had giggled like schoolgirls until after midnight.

Their great-grandfathers had ridden into British Columbia early in the century. One brother had ended up working at Fort Steele, but Robin's great-grandfather had remained in the wilderness to build a cabin and start a ranch.

Robin didn't mind that someone else now owned the property; in fact, she had been lucky enough to land a summer job there, thanks to Kathy. She couldn't wait to see the place she had heard about as a child, sitting at her grandmother's knee, entranced by stories of Sundance. But now...

She stopped pacing and shot a worried look up and down the road. There would be no job if she didn't get help, and quickly.

Suddenly a distant roar broke the silence, and she stepped to the edge of the road.

The oversized white truck didn't appear to be slowing down. Waving her arms to capture the driver's attention didn't seem to work either, so she bounded into the road in full view. "Please, God, an angel of mercy," she moaned.

As Craig Cameron gripped the wheel of his truck, demons of anger were pounding his brain. *What else could go wrong this year?* he wondered. He had thought he would never be happy again when Brenda died two years ago. It was as though every dream had been smashed. Then, in an effort to start a new life for himself and his young sons, he had left Washington and had bought a small ranch in British Columbia. An early snow had come before he got the hay up, sending him into winter short of feed. And that was only the beginning. The limited budget he had been operating on had dwindled fast, and by spring he had been forced to sell his cattle. The final blow had been the rage, or outrage, of his in-laws on a surprise visit to see their grandchildren. They had managed to plow through a March snowstorm in their four-wheel-drive truck, arriving unannounced on his doorstep.

"This is no place to raise the boys," Betsy Tillman had lashed out as she stumbled across the clutter-strewn living room, staring in horror. True to Craig's luck, it had been the day the boys were piled on the sofa, with runny noses and hacking coughs.

He stared absently at the highway, thinking about his future and that of his young sons. He seemed to have been cast into a dark tunnel that just grew deeper and colder with no light at the end. He still missed Brenda so much that the pain in his heart seemed, at times, unbearable. While it bothered him to give up his dream here, the dream had become empty without her.

The smell of sweet meadow grass drifted through the open window as his gaze swept the valley and climbed the Purcell Mountains. For a moment, serenity enveloped him like a breeze slipping over Clear Creek in the twilight of a summer afternoon. He had had the crazy notion that he could raise the boys on a ranch in Canada, away from crime and drugs and pollution. But with his savings dwindling, he might have to swallow his pride and accept his father-in-law's offer of a job.

He sighed. If he sold the ranch, he would be free of worrying about short growing seasons or rowdy ranch hands like Harley, the cook, who was laid up in town, waiting for the doctor to remove the cast from his leg. Despite his fifty-odd years, Harley had never lost his passion for rodeo, and during a weekend fiasco he had broken his leg. With Harley out, Craig needed someone to run the kitchen and watch the boys, which had led to the day's wild goose chase.

Craig's foot pressed harder on the accelerator as his frustration mounted. He should have been home long ago, and would have been if the new cook had arrived. Kathy, one of the tellers at the bank, had assured him that her cousin would be perfect for the job, that she was a competent schoolteacher who had cooked at the Calgary Stampede for years.

When he had asked her age, Kathy had reminded him that women don't like to tell their ages, but that Robin had been around long enough to handle the job. And she had taught in three different schools in the States! Craig hoped she wasn't too old to put up with two rambunctious boys.

He had given in for two reasons: he might need a loan from the bank before the month was out, and Kathy's father ran the bank. Now the woman had not shown up at the appointed time and place. After consuming a pot of coffee at the Caribou Café, he had stormed out.

Craig took the curve at his usual high speed, handling the big truck with competence. As the road opened again, he blinked in surprise, gripped the wheel tighter, and slammed on the brakes. It was not the sight of a car in the ditch that sent him skidding, but rather the woman standing directly in front of him. She whirled and sprinted to a gully after scaring the wits out of him and almost causing a wreck.

The big wheels ground against the paved road as the truck skidded momentarily while he pulled the steering wheel hard from side to side, then eased it back to center. He was almost too angry to stop; still, it went against his nature to pass up someone in need of help.

He eased the big truck over to the edge of the road and rolled down the window.

"Hi," a friendly-sounding voice called to him. He focused on a tall, slim woman with a tangle of golden-red hair, a greasy T-shirt, and snug jeans above dusty hiking boots. "I'm glad you stopped!"

"Didn't have much choice with you blocking the road," he retorted. His eyes lingered on her hair, and he found himself thinking of a Canadian sunrise, before a quick glance skimmed her slim figure and returned to her face. Her hazel eyes tilted upward at the corners, giving her a look of complete innocence. Those hazel eyes framed with black lashes would have stopped most men in their tracks. But not him. The agony of a broken heart had numbed his feelings toward women.

Robin's smile wobbled, then disappeared. If he didn't want to be friendly, fine. Maybe he was having a rough day, too. She needed to get out of the ditch, though, and the size of his truck gave her hope.

"What happened?" he asked, frowning back at her Toyota.

"I took the curve too wide and hit loose gravel on the edge," she said.

The man looked away, apparently doubting her innocence. Whatever questions he might have about her, clearly he wasn't about to ask. Without further comment, he sighed and reached for the door handle.

Robin shoved her hands into her jeans pockets and waited as the door opened and a pair of smooth leather boots, long denim legs, and a faded denim shirt led upward to a bronze face beneath a dark brown Stetson. Eyes as dark as mahogany bored through her. The thick hair beneath the Stetson was even darker.

She took a deep breath, trying to regain her scattered wits as he strode toward her, growing taller with each step. She tilted her head to look up at him, feeling the distinct pleasure of surveying a man who was not merely her height or shorter. This one was a couple of inches over six feet tall.

The man walked over to the blue Toyota. He leaned down to inspect the fender, then studied the car's angle in the ditch.

He looked back at her. "I can pull you out."

"You can? I really would appreciate it."

"The ditch isn't that deep," he said as he turned and hurried back to his truck.

Robin watched anxiously as he turned the truck around and pulled up in front of her car. He came out of the truck, holding a long coil of cable which he secured to the trailer hitch on his pickup. He straightened the cable down to her car.

"This'll work," he called, stretching out on his back to loop the cable around the axle of the Toyota.

Robin crossed and uncrossed her arms, staring at the long denim legs and fine leather boots now collecting the same dust she wore on her shirt.

"Okay," he said, wiggling out from under the car and dusting off his jeans as he stood. "Get in the car and put the gear shift in neutral. Be sure the brake is off," he added, walking back to his truck.

Robin sidled down the short incline of the ditch, opened the door of the Toyota, and got in. She felt as though she were climbing on a ride at a carnival as she slammed the door and surveyed the world from a lopsided angle.

As he cranked up the big truck, she hurriedly put the car in neutral and released the hand brake. Gripping the wheel with sweaty palms, she held on tight as the truck eased forward, cutting the slack in the cable. The truck moved again, its powerful engine drilling the silence. Her little car lurched up from the ditch and back onto the road.

"Thank God," Robin muttered, pushing the gear shift to park.

He was out of the truck, swiftly unwinding cable and then detaching the opposite end from her car. As he worked, she reached into her shoulder bag for her wallet. She could feel the bulk of the family pictures she carried pressing against the skinny side of the compartment that held the bills. A very few bills. She wondered what this man would say if he knew that her supply was about as pitiful as her Toyota. Nevertheless, she owed him.

"Try to keep it on the road," he called, the cable coiled neatly in his hand. He turned back to the truck.

"Wait!" Removing a twenty, she hopped out of the car. "Thanks," she said, extending the money.

He glanced from the crumpled bill to the woman. A look of amusement crept into his eyes but stayed away from his mouth. Standing close to him, she couldn't help noticing his features, handsomely carved and masculine. He would be perfect on one of those billboard ads, riding out across the range, or in a television commercial advertising some masculine cologne that only "real" men seemed to endorse. She just wished he wasn't so unfriendly.

"You don't owe me anything," he said quietly, then turned and walked back to his truck.

"But…" Robin stared after him, confused by the kindness that seemed so at odds with his stern expression. "Are you sure? I mean—" She faltered, wondering what she did mean. "Well, thanks for your help." Would a simple thank-you make any difference to this stern man?

"You're welcome," he said with a slam of his door. The engine snapped quickly to his command, sending a roar through the silence. He glanced back at her, and for a moment the hard line of his mouth softened into the semblance of a grin. "Be careful."

He turned the wheel, and the big truck made a wide U-turn in the highway and barreled east.

Robin stood in the center of the road, staring after him through the cloud of dust rolling over her like a brown wave. If he was the angel of mercy she had prayed for, he was a little short on mercy. *Doesn't matter,* she told herself, grateful he had stopped to help. At last she was out of that blasted ditch. She dashed back to her car and roared off.

Caribou Creek was a small settlement of wooden buildings strung along a wide place in the road. A few shops and a post

office comprised the town, along with a couple of filling stations with self-serve gas pumps out front. The life of the town
appeared to be the Caribou Café, a rustic-looking building with
a set of caribou antlers nailed to the sign out front. Robin
angled her little car past the pickups and four-wheel vehicles
and nosed into the last vacant parking space.

She cut the engine and quickly assessed her reflection in the
rear-view mirror. Her hair was a mess, most of her mascara was
gone, and only a trace of lip gloss remained in the center of her
bottom lip. Sighing, she finger-combed her layered hairdo and
bit her lips for instant color. She wasn't looking for a boyfriend
—she was interviewing for a job—so there was no point in
fussing over her plain appearance. She only needed to look
competent and sensible, and with that in mind, she reached
into the back seat and pulled a clean denim vest on over her
stained white T-shirt.

Running her tongue over even white teeth, she reached for
her shoulder bag and hopped out of the car.

The café was a long rectangle with red-checkered curtains
and tablecloths adding cheer to the knotty pine walls. At first
glance, the room was like a big homey kitchen, with tables and
chairs grouped together to accommodate half-a-dozen men in
jeans and work shirts. They had been engaged in lively conversation until one man looked her way and gawked. Then the
chatter faded to silence.

She glanced around the circle of men, wondering which one
was Craig Cameron. All eyes swept her boldly, bringing an
embarrassed flush to her cheeks. Behind the eating bar, a
woman scarcely tall enough to see over the counter was pouring coffee and flirting with the cowboy seated at the bar. They
were both in a fit of laughter over something she had said and
didn't hear the front door close. Then the woman noticed the

21

curious stares on the faces of the men at the tables, and she turned toward Robin, who lingered just inside the door.

The waitress blinked in surprise before her full lips split into a wide grin as she waved the coffeepot in greeting.

"Hi, there. Want some coffee?"

Robin smiled and hurried to the eating bar. "No, thanks." She leaned over the bar and lowered her voice. "I'm supposed to meet Craig Cameron here. Could you please point him out to me?"

Hazel Wallace cocked her head at an angle, looking Robin over a bit differently.

"Craig already left," she answered matter-of-factly.

Behind her, Robin could hear a few snorts followed by a buzz of whispers.

Hazel whirled and scowled at the men before placing the coffeepot back on the burner. She folded her arms on the edge of the counter and leaned toward Robin. This time she lowered her voice and phrased a tactful question.

"Are you, by chance, the new cook who's gonna take over for Harley? That sorry Harley." She was shaking her head, yet there was a curious twinkle in her dark eyes.

"I was supposed to meet Mr. Cameron here earlier, but I had car trouble," Robin explained, although the waitress hadn't asked.

Hazel nodded. "Well, he was pretty mad when he left here, so you better skedaddle on out to Sundance. Craig is..." She hesitated, then shrugged. "Well, he's kind of gruff sometimes, but he's had a rough time."

A new thought seemed to occur to her as she gave Robin another look. "You two never met?"

"No, my cousin in Cranbrook got me the job."

Hazel nodded. "Well, he could use some help, that's for

sure. And I have an idea you'll fill the bill just right. In fact, I just may have to hire Harley here when he's able to get around on those short legs of his!"

Robin was a bit surprised by this woman's confidence in her. Somehow it lifted her own sagging spirits. "Thanks. Can you give me directions to the ranch? Sundance?" She repeated the word slowly, glad none of the owners since her great-grandfather had bothered to change the name.

Hazel turned and looked across the room. "Sam?" she yelled. "Isn't it time for you to head back to the ranch? This gal needs someone to show her the way."

The clatter of an overturned chair brought Robin around in time to see a tall cowboy leaping to his feet as his friends snickered behind their coffee cups.

"I was just fixin' to leave," Sam answered, glaring at one cowboy who was muttering something to those seated at the table.

Robin felt her temper rising when the cowboys gave up trying to hide their amusement and a roar of laughter broke out.

"Don't mind these guys." Hazel shook her head, as though the cowboys were hopeless. "They're a little short on manners."

Sam, dressed in Levi's and a plaid shirt with pearl buttons, ambled toward her. Robin thought his expression was a mixture of pleasure and embarrassment as he gave her a lopsided grin.

"I need to get some gas first," Robin said, feeling self-conscious with all eyes pinned on her.

"You can do that across the street at Will's," he answered, placing his hat on his head.

"Stop in again," Hazel smiled at her.

"Thanks, I will."

Three

❦

Robin judged by her speedometer that she had trailed Sam's old pickup for at least twenty miles when his turn signal flashed beside a sign hand-painted in black letters; Sundance Road. Beneath the name, an arrow pointed toward the mountains.

Robin followed Sam onto a gravel road, narrow yet well maintained, running beside a log fence. The road led toward a cut in the mountain a mile away. Bordering the road on the left was a row of cottonwoods, and beyond the trees she could see a narrow creek tumbling over smooth rocks.

Ahead, the banks of the creek crossed a meadow lined with cottonwoods and willows. The creek and the road seemed to enter the mountains at the same place; it looked as though they would dead-end into the mountain. Then suddenly the road curled into a narrow gorge, and the valley pinched tighter. A high, rock-rimmed canyon enclosed the valley, just wide enough for the creek and road to pass through.

Again, the turn signal flashed as Sam exited from the road onto a cattle guard that served as a gate. Extending from one wall of the canyon to the other, a surprising, beautiful white fence closed off the gorge and creek and opened abruptly into a spectacular valley with evergreen mountains on both sides of the valley floor. The creek widened, stretching like a satin ribbon across half-mile-wide meadows.

About two hundred yards ahead, in an island of trees, she could see the ranch house, barn, and corrals. Robin's breath caught at the beauty of the panorama. On her right, two ten-foot-high posts with chains anchored a sign, exquisitely carved and rendered from an enormous tree trunk, that read SUN-DANCE. Bordering those words was the brand S/C.

Skook and Chuck, she thought, feeling her chest swell with pride. Her uncles had ridden in here and claimed this land; then, later, Skook had bought Chuck out. Still, it was a registered brand that had gone with the sale of the ranch.

Her heart beat faster as she gazed across the lush meadows and saw a dozen or more beautiful horses, their tails switching in the breeze. Robin thought she must have died and gone to heaven.

Sam's truck slowed as they approached the ranch house, centered at the north end of the valley to capture the sun. Constructed of weathered logs, the house appeared larger than its one story because of the high, steep-pitched roof, designed to shed heavy snow in winter. A front porch at least forty feet long stretched across the south end. Farther back, she could see a bunkhouse, barn, and feed lots. And she knew somewhere up this valley that narrowed again was the cabin built by Skook Russell, her great-grandfather.

Finally, she was here.

Sam's truck was pulling into a parking area. She pulled in beside him, cut the engine, and hopped from the car.

This was going to be wonderful, she thought, hurrying past Sam to the rock walkway leading to...

Her gaze fell on two small bodies on the front porch. What

was happening up there? Two little boys were pretzelled into a headlock, with neither one looking inclined to give an inch.

Robin thought the blond boy might be a couple of years younger than the brown-haired one. The little blond had just opened his mouth to sink his teeth into the other one's ear; she decided to speak up.

"No fair biting! Try a leg kick instead," Robin called out.

The younger one missed the ear and bit his own tongue at the sound of her voice.

Both scrambled loose and lunged to a sitting position, staring wide-eyed at Robin as she clapped her hands.

"Boy, you two are really good," she said, looking from one to the other.

The older boy tilted his head to the side, appraising her with an open mouth while the younger one gulped and blinked, then shouted a question to her.

"What do you know about fighting?"

"A lot! My sisters and I used to wrestle all the time. I usually won," Robin announced confidently.

Looking down at the two smudged faces, she felt a tug at her heartstrings. She adored children, particularly boys, since she had always wanted a brother. Her eyes rested first on the older boy with huge brown eyes and dark brown hair, then moved to the other, a blond with wide blue eyes that seemed to dance with mischief.

A door banged, and a man charged onto the porch. He looked as though he had just gotten up from a nap, since his hair was tousled and his dark eyes held a weary glaze. His shirt overhung his Levi's, and he had just begun stuffing the loose ends into his waistband when he stopped short, blinking and staring at her. Robin gasped: it was the man who had helped her on the road. She felt her brain stall.

Sam, who had been lingering somewhere in the background chuckling, was the first to speak.

"Mr. Cameron, I brought the lady out. She had car trouble. That's why she was late to meet you at the café."

Looking pleased with himself for straightening things out, Sam strolled off to the bunkhouse, and Robin stared after him for a moment. Then she let her eyes drift slowly back to Mr. Cameron, wondering how he would take the news that she had been unable to deliver.

He did not take it well.

Robin watched first shock then horror seize his features. His eyes turned black as midnight, and she inwardly cringed and turned back to the boys, eager for a change of subject.

"How old are you two?"

Before they could answer, Craig had reached her side in a few hasty steps and frowned down at her.

"You're the cook?" he rasped.

She took a deep breath and forced herself to face him squarely. "The fact that I misjudged that curve has nothing to do with the way I cook. And I assure you, I *can* cook."

"It doesn't matter," he brushed her words aside. "I need someone who can also look after the boys—"

"I'd love to," she said, quickly sidestepping him. Craig had clearly recovered from his shock, and she sensed he would simply want to get rid of her. She must be too young and attractive to match what he had expected in a cook and caregiver for the boys.

She turned to the brothers, who appeared to be at a loss for words. "What are your names?" she asked.

Will took a step forward, as though assuming his role as big brother. "I'm Will, and this is Zack. I'm eight."

"And I'm six," Zack bellowed. "Can you ride a horse?"

Robin put a hand on her hip and pretended to be insulted.

27

"Why, of course I can ride a horse!"

"Do you—"

"Never mind, Zack," his father cut him short. "Look, er—"

"Robin Grayson. But you and the boys can call me Robin."

He frowned. "I'm afraid this won't work out," he said in a rush. "Harley—that's the cook who broke his leg—"

"He was riding in a rodeo," Zack informed her.

"Miss Grayson," his father said, interrupting him with mild but audible irritation. Zack turned to him curiously.

"I need a cook," his father continued, "a housekeeper, and a babysitter all in one. I don't think you want the job."

Zack looked back at Robin to see how she would take that.

Robin arched an eyebrow and regarded him coolly. "What you're saying is you don't think I can handle it. Honestly, I can. I'm an elementary school teacher, and I enjoy kids. Quite frankly, I like children better than adults most of the time."

She watched his dark eyes roll over her, then skid toward the boys. "Actually, I need someone who is, er, older."

"And you're younger than I expected," Robin retorted smoothly. "Are you the owner of this ranch or just the manager?"

"Dad bought it," Will volunteered.

Craig Cameron shook his head. This meeting was way out of control. He had Robin's attention again, though. "Exactly how much experience have you had cooking?"

"I learned to cook when I was twelve years old. And I cooked at the Calgary Stampede for years."

Craig eyed her suspiciously. He suspected her "cooking" duties had consisted of stirring the hot dog relish while entertaining a bunch of wide-eyed cowboys. This time he held his tongue, however, because Zack had inched his way up to her and was now boldly looking her over. Aware that his youngest son was about to ask a hundred questions, Craig knew he had to cut this encounter short. Unfortunately, the woman was standing her ground, to his mounting frustration.

"Can you make cookies?" Zack asked. "Harley can't make cookies. He—"

"Zack, you and Will have something to do inside," Craig interrupted. "When I passed your door, neither bed was made. You know the rules—"

"I don't wanna—"

"I want those beds made up now." Craig had not raised his voice, and yet the tone was firm enough to command action.

The boys exchanged glances and hurried for the door, but there Zack turned back. "What kind of cookies?" he yelled.

"Any kind you want."

Craig cleared his throat, hoping to drown out her pleasant voice, but the boys had already heard and were grinning as they dashed down the hall.

Craig turned back to face Robin, who had taken a seat in one of the porch rockers and was patiently waiting for him to make his speech. Chewing the inside of his bottom lip, he decided there would be no speech, no series of apologies or excuses. He'd simply tell her, straight out, that she wasn't right for the job.

His eyes lingered on her upturned face as some part of his brain registered the friendly expression in her hazel eyes, the quick easy smile, and her comfortable, unassuming manner. She actually seemed like a very nice woman, even though a bit scatterbrained, but none of that mattered. He wasn't going to hire her. It just wouldn't work out.

"Your boys are great," she said pleasantly.

He cleared his throat. "Thank you. They've gotten a bit out of hand recently. Their mother...that is, my wife, Brenda...died two years ago."

29

Robin stared at him, suddenly feeling sad for both the man and his sons. "I'm terribly sorry. I knew you and the boys were alone, but I didn't realize..." She faltered momentarily, wondering why Kathy hadn't explained this to her. To bridge the awkward silence, she glanced toward the mountains and asked a different sort of question.

"Is the old Russell cabin still standing?"

"The Russell cabin?"

She nodded. "Skook Russell's place." She stared thoughtfully at the snowcapped peaks at the far end of the valley.

"It's about three miles up there," he pointed.

She turned her eyes in that direction and stared in fascination.

"Why are you asking?" he inquired.

Robin gazed up the valley for several seconds more before turning back to explain. "Skook Russell was my great-grandfather."

She enjoyed delivering this little surprise and watching Craig's face as she spoke. His dark brows hiked; his eyes widened. "And you've never been to this part of the country?"

She shook her head. "No, I grew up in Calgary hearing all sorts of adventure stories about this place from my grandmother, who was born in that cabin. I guess the land has changed hands a few times since they lived here." Her eyes wandered over him, and she found herself very curious about this man and his sons.

Craig nodded as the frown between his dark brows deepened in contemplation. "Before I bought Sundance, folks tried to make a go of it as a working ranch, but there have always been problems."

"Such as?"

30

"There isn't enough meadowland and the summers are too short for raising the amount of hay needed to feed cattle."

She sighed. "That's too bad. It's beautiful here." Robin's eyes were drawn to the mountains once again. "After Skook died," she said, "my great-grandmother moved back home to Saskatchewan. She wanted Grandmother to have a good education."

Craig crossed his arms and looked at her. "What happened to the rest of your family?"

"Well, my grandmother married a wheat farmer, and my mother was one of four children raised on the prairies. Mom met Dad in college. After they were married, they moved to Calgary, and my two sisters and I were raised there. And now," her eyes twinkled, "you have the history of Skook Russell's descendants."

Craig had listened interestedly as his eyes slipped over the woman on his front porch. She wore little makeup and dressed like a cowgirl, in contrast to Brenda, who had been a striking blond who preferred soft sweaters and flowing skirts. And yet Robin Grayson was pretty in another way. There was a healthy glow to her skin and a sparkle in those hazel eyes. Nicely curved lips tilted easily in a cute little smile.

Craig pressed his back against the porch post and reminded himself she wouldn't fit in here. Still, he was beginning to see another side to her, making it more difficult for him to send her away. Naturally, he had heard lots of stories about Skook Russell, who blazed the first trail into this area when it was no more than a wilderness. When Skook died, his widow had sold the ranch and moved back east with their only child.

Robin broke into his thoughts. "Look, I just want a little time to explore, to go look around the cabin where my great-grandparents lived." She took a deep breath as her eyes pled

31

with his. "Please give me a chance to do that."

After talking with her, he could see she was intelligent and sensible, and she had certainly been direct with him about everything. Maybe this arrangement would be suitable for a short while, but only a short while. And even that depended on how she worked out.

Craig took a deep breath. How could he refuse? Maybe she could do the work, after all. And if she was related to the Russells...

"All right," he agreed. "But I'd like to hire you on a temporary basis. If things aren't working out after a week, I'll give you a week's severance pay, and you can still go exploring. Is that fair?"

She extended her hand. "Yes, that's fair."

Hesitantly, he accepted her handshake, feeling a strength in the slim fingers that surprised him.

"Now, where's the kitchen?" she asked, withdrawing her hand and coming to her feet again.

He took a deep breath. Earlier in the day, he would never have believed he would be hiring the woman who had almost caused him to wreck the truck. But given the circumstances, how could he refuse?

"Come on in," he said. "I'll show you around." And for the first time, a small grin kicked at one corner of his mouth before he could squelch it—almost a reflex, as if he was too serious about his hard life to be charming.

He didn't see Robin's surprised smile as she followed him into the house.

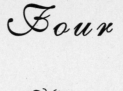

Four

T his house was built in the late forties by a wealthy couple from Idaho," Craig explained as they entered a large, cathedral-style living room and dining room combination. Near the center of the room a large rock fireplace held a few ashes, and the woodbox beside it was filled with logs.

"You have fires in the summer?" She glanced at Craig.

"Sometimes the evenings turn cool. We had snow here on the first of June. Since the fireplace is the main source of heat for this part of the house, we use it a lot. The hall leads back to the bedrooms."

"What's up there?" She pointed toward the ladder on the end wall, leading to a loft.

"The boys use it as a playroom. And they sleep there a lot in the winter, since it's the warmest place in the house."

Robin nodded. "I guess so." She looked over the living room again. "Your furniture is nice," she said, admiring the plaid overstuffed sofa and matching chairs. A large maple coffee table overflowed with games, and magazines were piled on the end tables beneath brass lamps. Western artwork lined the walls, along with a huge bookcase crammed with books, all sizes and shapes. Some leatherbound classics had been sandwiched between a series of children's books and a set of encyclopedias.

Robin's eyes moved back to the rock fireplace, and she imagined cheery fires while snowflakes feathered past the plate glass windows on the front.

"You may have already noticed," Craig was saying, "there's no television. Since the kids overdosed on TV in the States, I decided to wait a while before investigating the possibilities of a satellite dish."

"What a good idea," Robin answered, drawing a surprised look from him. "I was complaining to another teacher this past year about students who watch television rather than read. We only had one television set when I was growing up, and then my parents censored the programs. I thought they were very old-fashioned," she laughed, "but as a result I developed a passion for reading."

Craig frowned. "Will reads, but Zack won't sit still long enough. And by the way, there's no telephone."

Her mouth fell open. "Now *that* is hard to imagine."

"A ringing telephone has always driven me straight up the wall," he said, shaking his head as though frustrated by the memory. "I'm looking into one of the new cellular phones. I suppose I need a telephone, although I do have a short-wave radio in my room. I could get helicopter service right away in an emergency."

"That's good to know," she said, recalling the wrestling match on the front porch.

"I'll show you the kitchen," he said, leading the way through the dining area, centered with a huge table and chairs, to the wide end of an L-shaped kitchen.

"Since the houses up here were built before generators, the

34

women wanted their kitchens on the east side," Craig was saying.

Robin nodded. "To take advantage of the early morning light and warm sunshine."

She walked ahead of him, tracing a finger over the smooth wood grain of a large cupboard. She came up short at the gas stove, recalling a disaster with one she had used at a friend's house. Pushing that thought aside, she looked around the counters again. No microwave, of course.

Craig walked to the kitchen window and pointed to a small building forty feet away, between the main house and the bunkhouse. "That's where the generator is located. It's our sole source of electricity here."

He walked to the hallway, flipped a switch, and the kitchen light came on.

"Naturally, it runs a lot in the winter, but in the summer, I usually switch it on first thing in the morning to help the refrigeration, then cut it off until later. The days are long now, so we don't need lights until late."

She nodded, listening. "That's the quietest generator I ever heard. My dad took the family to a fish camp up in northern Alberta six years ago. Every morning someone had to trudge out in the cold to start the thing up, and boy did it roar!"

Craig nodded. "Yeah, this one used to be that way. Then I did some updating on it. I rigged up a two-way switch that works off a battery. I keep the battery charged so that all I have to do is flip the switch there in the hall."

Robin peered into the hall, locating the switch.

"As for it being quieter than the one you know about, I ran the exhaust at the back of the generator through another exhaust underground and out the back side. That dulls the sound even more; in fact, you won't even hear it unless you're outside."

She smiled. "You seem to have thought of everything."

His eyes locked with hers for a full second before he turned and looked around the kitchen.

"So, think you can manage here?" he asked.

"I'll do my best."

Something in his eyes told her he had his doubts, but she forced a bright smile, trying to look as though everything was just perfect.

Halfway down the hall, Craig stopped to point out a cubicle that contained a small woodburning heater. "This is closest to the guest bedroom," he indicated the room across the hall. "You'll be using that one. And your bath is here." He opened another door. "This was once a small bedroom, but I converted it to an extra bath. Is this okay for you?"

She glanced in. "Looks fine."

"The boys and I have adjoining bedrooms back there." He inclined his head toward the two closed doors farther down the hall. "Well," he shifted from one boot to another, "do you want to get settled in your room?"

She smiled. "Sure. I'll get my duffel bag."

"I'll help—"

"No, it's okay," she answered quickly. "I can manage."

Just then, something crashed to the floor in the next bedroom. The boys' voices rose in a heated argument, sending Craig off to settle another dispute.

Robin went back to the car for her bag. Her hand lingered on her guitar in its leather case. Should she take it in as well? Why not? Grabbing both, she retraced her steps into the house. Down the hall, she could hear Craig talking in a smooth-yet-firm tone. Although unable to hear what he was saying, she could tell that he was trying to straighten out the problem, whatever it was, in a sensible manner.

She turned into the guest room and looked around. The bedroom suite was a sturdy wood with a thick floral comforter and matching drapes, which were drawn. The closet was narrow, yet it was large enough to accommodate her on this brief stay. Maybe a very brief stay, she thought, recalling that he had only given her a week to prove herself.

Well, a week would be long enough. She sighed, opening her duffel bag and hanging clothes in the closet. She filled only the two top drawers of the chest. She'd love a bath, but that could wait. For now she'd better be thinking about her cooking duties. She changed clothes, stepping into clean jeans and a pale denim shirt, short-sleeved with deep chest pockets.

She brushed her hair until it gleamed bright red-gold, settling into smooth fringes around her face. Satisfied that she was ready for work, Robin returned to the kitchen and looked around again.

Everything was clean and in place, and yet the touch of a woman was obviously missing in the lack of frills or even little niceties. It was merely a plain, serviceable kitchen.

Her thoughts drifted toward the woman in the family picture on a table in the living room. Craig hadn't mentioned her, but Robin couldn't help noticing what a pretty woman Brenda had been, with nice features set off by blond hair and blue eyes.

Pushing her thoughts toward the meal, she opened the refrigerator and poked around. It appeared to be well stocked with the essentials, but the only meat she spotted was something neatly sliced and soaking in a small bowl of milk. She frowned. What sort of concoction was that?

Just then, Craig's footsteps sounded in the hallway, and he entered the kitchen. One corner of his shirt overhung his waistband again, as though he had been prying the boys apart or cleaning up a major mess.

"I was going to fry elk for supper," he said, looking toward the open door of the refrigerator. "But you probably can't do that, so—"

"Yes, I can." The words were out of her mouth before she could stop them, and it had to be either ignorance or pride, she would later reason, that made her blurt such a thing.

He stared at her while she willed herself not to back down. "Are you sure?" The question was like a challenge, and that made her even more determined.

She cleared her throat. "If you'll just show me where you keep the flour and skillets and—"

He was already opening a cabinet, pulling down a ten-pound sack of flour and a five-gallon container of cooking oil.

"I see you buy in quantity," she said, looking from the flour and oil to the huge cast iron skillet he was removing from a cabinet beside the stove.

He glanced over his shoulder. "I have to stock up when I go into town, otherwise…" His voice trailed as he placed the big skillet on the stove, then turned back to her. "I usually cook rice to go with the meat and gravy."

Gravy? She merely blinked and nodded. "I like rice."

They stared at each other for a long moment before he shoved his hands in his pockets and started for the door. "If there's nothing else—"

"I can manage just fine," she assured him, her hands clasped together, her fingers tightly laced.

"I'll leave the generator going," he said, lingering in the doorway. His eyes still looked grim. When she turned around and went to work, he finally gave up and walked out.

I can do this, she told herself with a sigh as she walked to the stove and stared blankly at the huge cast iron skillet. *It will just take time and patience.* There was no need to fuss about cholesterol or her distaste for fried foods at this point. On her first night here, she would try and do things his way. *After tonight, I'll start preparing healthy dishes,* she promised herself.

The rice. She made a search with the cabinet doors banging loudly behind her. She came upon a five-pound sack of rice and shook her head. Either he rarely went to town, or he lived in fear of being snowbound. She tried not to think of the implications of that as she went to the sink to wash her hands.

"What're you fixin' for supper?" a voice whispered just under her elbow.

She jumped, spraying water and bringing a delighted giggle from Zack.

"How about fried elk?" she asked, wiping her hands on a cup towel.

"Yippee," he shouted.

"Zack," Craig called from the doorway, "come on to the barn with me. You and Will have some duties. And we need to leave Miss Grayson alone so she can cook."

Footsteps made hollow echoes over the hardwood floors until the front door banged and the house was blissfully quiet.

Robin took a deep breath. *I can do this,* she repeated.

Half an hour later, she had managed to light one of the gas burners and put the rice, water, and seasonings in a pan on the stove. Now she was battering the meat strips in flour and had poured a generous amount of oil into the skillet. How much oil would it take? she wondered, frowning back at the meat. The truth was, she had never fried anything in her life. She had become a health nut in her teens and rarely ate meat, but when she did she chose baked chicken or fish.

"When in Rome, do as the Romans do," she muttered, remembering her mom's words.

She peered down into the skillet, half filled with oil. She

frowned. It was a big skillet. And deep. She added more oil until the skillet was three quarters full.

She set about looking for dish towels and pot holders. She located one gloved pot holder which looked about three sizes too big for her hand. She turned back to the floured meat, moving the bowl next to the skillet.

Taking a deep breath, she turned on the other gas burner and watched as a tiny flame wavered. She waited a few more minutes, watching with satisfaction as the heat from the burner rose up, warming her face. Peering into the skillet, she saw the oil was beginning to smoke, so she assumed it was time to put the meat in to fry.

She had dropped several pieces of meat into the skillet when she realized her mistake: there was too much oil, the skillet was too hot, and it was going to overflow if she added one more piece of meat. She bit her lip, wondering what to do.

Perspiration gathered on her upper lip as she fought a stab of panic. She had to get the skillet off the burner. *Let the oil cool down, then pour off at least a cupful.*

With that in mind, she shoved her hand into the huge potholder and lifted the skillet. Her hand began to tremble beneath the weight. Her left hand shot over to support her right wrist, but the damage was already done. A trickle of hot grease had overflowed the skillet and was splashing over her arm.

She screamed before she could stop herself, and now all she could think of was getting the skillet back down on the stove, even though more drops of hot oil threatened to splash onto the burner.

Her upper teeth sank into her bottom lip as she tried not to think about her burned arm and attempted to still her trembling hands.

She heard steps whisking over the floor, and then a pair of

strong arms came around her, reaching for the handle of the skillet.

"Here, let me."

She darted a glance up and saw that Craig was calmly taking the skillet from her hands and carefully maneuvering it toward the sink. Then he turned off the burner.

Robin's eyes dropped to her arm. Hot oil still gleamed just above her wrist, and the skin was bright red. It was throbbing so badly she wanted to cry. But if she dared let tears form, it would be over her stupidity. Her breath jerked in her chest as she lifted her eyes to Craig, waiting for him to turn around and start fussing about how she could have burned the house down.

He said nothing as he grabbed a cup towel and gently began to swab her arm. He studied her face, as though trying to see if she was in pain, but she kept her expression calm as she lowered her eyes, ashamed to face him.

"I keep a first-aid kit in the cabinet," he said. "Just take a seat at the table, and I'll grab it."

Robin nodded, saying nothing. As she slumped into the chair, she viewed the trail of disaster. Clumps of flour had been scattered along the countertops during her session of battering, and there were more on the floor, along with spilled milk on the countertop. In the sink, the smoke rolled up from the skillet, and she thought she could hear a dull sizzle. The oil was so hot it was still cooking the meat without the heat of the stove.

She sighed and inspected her wrist. It looked as though it had been parboiled and was one step beyond rare. She sighed, closing her eyes while Craig moved quickly around, opening and closing a door, adeptly gathering up what he needed. He pulled a chair close to hers and placed a large metal box on the table. She stared at it dully.

"Our first-aid kit," he said. He spoke in a gentle voice and didn't seem to mind his new role as paramedic. "I have bits and pieces of everything in here." He plowed through the box. "What we need now is that burn cream I just bought."

She took a deep breath and slowly looked up at his face. She met dark eyes that drifted over her features, then back to her eyes. She blinked twice, searching for the right words. Since she felt like a complete fool, she found it difficult to think of anything at all to say in her defense.

"Come on," he said, rising. "Let's get it under cold water first." He led her to the sink and gently turned on the icy water. She winced and he glanced at her with concern. After a few minutes, they sat down again.

"I'll try to take it easy," he said, directing his attention to her arm. "This is bound to sting a bit."

"It's okay." She pinned her gaze to the strong masculine hand that held her arm while his other hand gingerly dabbed her wet skin dry and then swabbed a thick salve over her burned skin. She gritted her teeth against the stinging that penetrated the nerve endings.

"Could have been worse," he assured her. "I think it's a minor burn, although it probably doesn't feel that way now. I'll put lots of ointment on it, but we won't use any gauze just yet. It needs to air dry."

"Thank you," she said in a weak voice. "I'll be fine."

She was looking at his thick hair as he bent over her arm. She could smell a wonderful spicy something. She wasn't sure if it was a cologne or a pine scent from outdoors that clung to him, but she liked it, whatever it was.

Her eyes sneaked from his head to the broad shoulders that stretched his denim shirt. It was unnerving to have her employer so close to her, doctoring her arm. Her eyes roamed down his long arms to his square hands, darkly tanned. Watching his long fingers move as gently as silk over her burning skin, she felt her nerves coiling again.

She swallowed, suspiciously aware that she was attracted to this man, which only added to her problems. There was no way she could let herself think of him in any way other than employer, and he probably wouldn't be her employer much longer. In fact, she had better be thinking of the right words to convince him to let her stay another day. She'd really like to borrow a horse and ride over to the Russell cabin.

"I think it's going to be okay," he said, repacking the first-aid kit.

He was speaking to her with a gentleness that surprised her, and she was touched by his concern.

"Mr. Cameron, I know what you must be thinking, and I don't blame you," she said in a weary voice.

"What am I thinking?" The dark eyes held a glint of amusement as he snapped the kit and looked back at her.

Robin's eyes locked with his. There was an expression of kindness, maybe even tenderness. She was puzzled. When she expected him to be polite, he was rude; when she expected him to be angry, he was kind. Craig Cameron was a very difficult man to understand.

Craig found that he did not understand himself, either. He had not been angry with her; he only felt sorry for her. He had looked into the large hazel eyes, seen the embarrassment and humiliation, and felt a stab of sympathy. He was not an I-told-you-so man, never had been.

As they stared at one another for several seconds, he felt a smile pulling at his lips. Since smiles rarely touched his lips these days, he seemed to have forgotten how to use those muscles. But something about her made him want to smile.

"What you must be thinking," Robin finally picked up her train of thought, "is that you shouldn't have listened to Kathy, or to me. That you were right about my cooking."

He shrugged lightly, glancing back at the skillet. "I don't know about your cooking. The meat isn't done yet. Looks like you knew how to batter it okay though, and the rice you put on earlier is smelling good. Maybe what you don't know how to do is deal with a gas stove, and I admit it can be tricky." He stood up, hands on hips, frowning at the stove. "I probably should get a new one."

"It wasn't the stove," Robin sighed. "I just—"

"Listen, why don't I finish up the meal? With that arm, you don't need to be doing anything."

"I can handle the rice and set the table."

"Okay, if you want to. And I'll manage the rest."

With that, they both went to work. Craig drained some of the grease from the skillet, toweled off the outside, and lit the burner again. Neither spoke as they moved about their duties, but he noticed that Robin was keeping an eye on the way he fried the meat, turning the strips until they were a crisp, golden brown, then draining them on a platter with two thicknesses of paper towels.

So her confidence about frying elk was partly a bluff, as he had suspected. She kept watching as he finished with the meat and made gravy. He had drained the grease, leaving only the brown sediments and adding extra flour. He browned the flour and added a generous dash of salt and pepper, then poured hot water into the skillet. A plume of steam rose up.

Robin backed up reflexively, but he was too adept to allow spills. He stirred the contents with an expert hand, blending the mixture smoothly before adding milk and finally pulling a skillet full of rich brown gravy from the stove. He set it on a wooden trivet, then turned to Robin.

"I'll just go and have the boys wash up for supper." As he headed down the hall, he felt that smile tugging at his mouth again.

Why did he need to hire a cook? Robin asked herself. She was in awe. Nobody could improve on his skill.

By the time she poured milk into tall glasses and sliced some apples onto a dessert plate, the kitchen was filled with wonderful aromas. As the boys got ready, Robin surveyed the table set for four, with strips of meat fried to golden brown perfection, rich brown gravy, and a huge bowl of rice. She found herself experiencing again that wonderful sense of a family gathering to share a meal. It was one of the things she had missed so much over the years, that unity at mealtime, sharing events of the day, enjoying food and fellowship.

As the boys bolted into the kitchen, then slowed down to regard both Robin and the food, she smiled at them.

"Your father has prepared a wonderful meal."

"I thought you were the cook!" Zack shouted.

"Not tonight. I had a little problem."

"You burned your arm," Will said quietly, frowning at the red splotch of skin.

"It's nothing serious. I just learned a good lesson about not filling a skillet too full of grease."

"Are you gonna quit?" Zack asked, his eyes narrowing.

She hesitated, wondering if she should be gracious enough to offer a resignation, but she didn't really want to do that. Not yet.

"No, Zack, she isn't quitting. Now get to eating and stop pestering Miss Grayson."

Robin hesitated as everyone else reached for their forks. Craig glanced at her. "Is something wrong?"

"Would you mind if I say grace?" she asked, glancing at the boys.

"Mom always said grace," Will said, staring into his plate.

Craig cleared his throat. "Go ahead."

"God, thank you for this food and bless it to the nourishment of our bodies and our bodies to thy service." She hesitated, filled with more thoughts of praise, but then decided to cut it short. "In Jesus' name, Amen."

"I know one," Zack yelled. "Want me to say it?"

"You can say it next time," his father answered quietly. "Shall we eat?"

Robin tried to control the little smile forming in the corners of her mouth. It would be so easy to get attached to these boys, and even to the man. Her eyes slid to him. He ate in silence, his brow furrowed again, his thoughts seemingly miles away.

While she had worried about getting in the way, it now appeared he didn't even notice she was there. She suppressed a sigh. At least he hadn't used her disaster with the skillet to remind her she couldn't handle the job. He was giving her another chance—and this time she wasn't going to disappoint him.

Five

Craig stood on the porch, looking up at the mountains scalloped against the sky. The boys were finally in bed, and Robin Grayson had gone to her room and closed the door. He had busied himself with his ledgers all evening so that he could avoid her. She hadn't seemed to notice, however, as she entertained the boys with stories of the Calgary Stampede.

Shoving his hands in his pockets, he took the steps two at a time and began to walk aimlessly across the yard.

Ever since that woman had said grace at the dinner table, his conscience had been nagging him. Brenda had taken the boys to church, but he had always been too busy to go with them, or so he told her.

His gruff exterior had almost become routine. He worked hard to keep his tender heart a secret. Although Brenda teasingly labeled him a big teddy bear, she had always appreciated his tenderness. Before he got into ranching, he had worked briefly for a hard-nosed boss who demanded that his salespeople be as tough as nails. He was ready to fire Craig when Craig resigned on his own and went back to doing what he loved—working with horses on a friend's ranch.

Growing up as the youngest of three children, Craig had been the one who worried about feed for the birds when it snowed. And he wanted to keep every homeless animal that strayed into his yard. Once, as a child, he had sobbed behind the house when a sparrow's nest had blown down and all the hatchlings died.

His brothers teased him, and his father tried to prod him into hiding his tears. *Gotta be tough,* they'd admonished. But his mother drew him to her and hugged him. She understood because she had the same heart.

He had ended up at the corral, and now he stood with his arms crossed over the fence. He stared into the darkness, hearing the comforting neigh of Chief, his big sorrel. That sound was a balm to his troubled senses as he tilted his head back and gazed toward the soft starry sky.

He was drawn like a magnet to the wide open spaces of British Columbia, the spectacular mountains, the clear rushing streams. He remembered the day he had found Sundance—it had been the only thing in the world that seemed to comfort the boys and him after losing Brenda.

He would miss this land, and it hurt to give up on a dream. But he had no choice.

Glancing back toward the house, he saw the light in the window of the guest bedroom and he thought of the woman who had come. Robin Grayson. He had felt sorry for her because she had seemed so helpless with that skillet of grease. But now she was probably thinking he didn't care if she could cook or not, that she could manipulate him into letting her stay on after the way she and her cousin had tricked him into thinking he was hiring an older, matronly housekeeper. And that nagged at his pride.

A muscle in his jaw clenched as he turned his gaze from the

window. Well, she'd find out that this was a business arrangement, nothing more. And if her cooking didn't improve in the next day or two, he would have no choice but to fire her.

The lamp on the nightstand cast a soft glow on the worn pages of the Bible that lay open in Robin's lap. She had just finished reading the eighty-fourth Psalm, one of Granny's favorites. Thoughtfully, she turned back to the inside cover of the Bible, a gift from Granny, whose mother, Jenny Russell, had owned it first. Granny had given it to Robin on her tenth birthday. She read the verse inscribed by Jenny Russell inside the cover.

"For the LORD God is a sun and shield: the LORD will give grace and glory: no good thing will he withhold from them that walk uprightly—Psalm 84:11."

Smiling sadly, she closed the Bible and stared at the cover, worn and frayed in places. Still, she had chosen not to replace the cover. The years and the use of the Bible made it extra special to her.

"Jenny Russell, what would you think if you knew I was staying on Russell land tonight?" she asked softly.

Automatically, her eyes drifted toward the ceiling, and the wistful smile widened into a happy one.

"You do know, don't you?" she whispered into the silence.

She lay very still, relishing all the feelings that flowed through her. Then she gently placed the Bible on the nightstand and turned out the light. Punching her pillow, she snuggled down under the covers.

Through a crack in the drapes, she could see the sky, and it looked as though a million silver stars had been sprinkled onto a black velvet canvas. As the night's soft silence wrapped around her, she breathed a contented sigh. It amazed her that she felt so comfortable here, almost at home, despite her rather puzzling employer.

She tried not to think of him; instead, she thought of Will and Zack. They had kept their distance from her throughout the evening, even though she had tried to win their friendship. Zack had alternated between laughing at her stories, then challenging her with an I-don't-believe-you. Will had held back, watching her thoughtfully with wide dark eyes that seemed to reflect a keen intelligence. Zack's eyes darted here and there while he fidgeted. At times, he didn't seem to know or care what she was saying, which wasn't unusual for a boy his age. But then he had become attentive again when she spoke of the Calgary Stampede, looking entranced. Will, on the other hand, seemed interested in everything.

She snuggled lower under the comforter as bone-deep weariness began to creep through her. She was exhausted physically, but her mind kept circling the situation here—the ranch, the boys, their father. She flexed her wrist, relieved that the burned skin was healing after the gentle care she had received from Craig Cameron.

Her eyelids drifted down as sleep edged into her consciousness. Her last thoughts were of eyes as black as the night beyond her window and a feather-light touch that was at odds with the gruff man she had met on the road.

The house was perfectly quiet as Robin dragged herself from the comfort of her bed. Frowning at her travel clock, she saw that morning came early at Sundance.

It was only 8:00 A.M. Saturday, but apparently someone was up. She heard a cabinet door bang somewhere in the house. She reached for her silk robe and pulled it on over her pajamas. Wandering to the window, she peered out. She had a view of the barn and corrals and an edge of the mountain range beyond.

While thrusting her feet into her house shoes, she thought about the climate in Charleston. It would be hot and muggy there, while here the temperature might climb to the eighties but at least the evenings were pleasant and cool and the air was dry.

She turned to face her reflection in the mirror and met a pair of hazel eyes peering from swollen sockets. She had slept hard in her new surroundings, and now she was probably running late for breakfast.

Cracking the door, she peered across the hall and saw that the bathroom was empty.

Crossing to the hall, she came face to face with Zack, still in his pajamas, a box of cereal hugged against his chest. Seeing her, he jumped, spilling cereal on the floor. Wide-eyed, he turned to glare at her.

This was one uptight kid, she thought, giving him a friendly smile while resisting a sudden urge to hug him. Her instincts told her he wasn't ready for that. Her eyes slipped over him, taking in his disheveled appearance. The cowlick at his crown stood straight up, while the rest of his blond hair toppled over his sleep-filled eyes. His little face needed a warm washcloth, she noted; he had obviously crawled out of bed and headed for the cereal.

"How are you this morning?" she asked pleasantly, bending down to help clean up the cereal.

"Terrible."

"Sorry to hear it."

"You scared me!" he grumbled as he trudged back to his room and slammed the door.

"Sorry," she said, flipping the switch to turn on the generator. Then she hurried into the bathroom.

After a quick bath, she dressed in fresh jeans and a T-shirt and headed toward the kitchen.

Zack had returned and was standing before the living room window, staring out.

"Zack," she called gently. As he turned with a frown, she asked, "Where's your brother?"

"Gone to the barn with Dad." He dipped his hand into the cereal box and came up with a handful which he popped in his mouth. Well, that was one way to eat cereal, she thought, heading toward the kitchen.

So, Craig Cameron was already at work. *What time am I expected to get up?* she wondered, feeling a bit guilty. She should have bought another alarm clock, she decided, knowing it would probably get tossed with a malicious sense of glee, just like the last one.

She was not, by nature, an early riser, but she knew that would have to change if she stayed here. Her new employer probably expected her to bolt out of bed at the crack of dawn and get breakfast on the table. The idea was not appealing to her, but she would merely think of it as a challenge, a game—and she loved games.

The smell of coffee still lingered in the air as she entered the kitchen. A huge metal pot, smoke-stained and slightly dented, sat on the cold stove. When she picked up the pot, she heard the slosh of coffee. Carefully, she turned on the gas burner and placed the coffeepot on it.

She glanced at the dishes in the sink. One large bowl, one medium-sized bowl. So Craig and Will had eaten cereal earlier and headed out to do chores, no doubt.

Okay, so she'd messed up on another meal. Strike two. Well, she'd get a jump on lunch and have it on the table in time and in perfect order, if that meant starting right now.

Turning on the faucet and dribbling liquid detergent into the sink, she decided there was no harm in letting the dishes soak while she grabbed a bowl of cereal herself.

A search of the cabinets turned up everything but cereal, so she ventured back to the living room.

"Zack, could I have some cereal, please?" She reached out to touch his shoulder lightly.

He shrugged away from her touch, dumping out more cereal.

"There's not any left," he said, hugging the box.

She decided to ignore the lie in the interest of improving their testy relationship. She walked around and knelt beside the sofa, scooping up the spilled cereal.

"Fine," she smiled, popping one of the Cheerios in her mouth and strolling back to the kitchen.

She felt his eyes trailing her. She had a feeling that his mother would never have eaten food that had been dropped on the floor. But she had already decided to treat the boys as equals, without passing judgment on their manners. Would that be possible? she wondered as she stood in the kitchen, staring thoughtfully into space. Zack was obviously in need of a mother's guidance. But her job was cooking, she reminded herself, eyeing a loaf of bread and contemplating toast.

Just then the back door slammed and Will entered the kitchen, followed by his father. Both were dressed similarly—jeans and T-shirts—but the expressions on their faces were quite a contrast. Will had a look of mild curiosity in his dark eyes, while his father wore a surly frown as he looked at her.

Robin's good humor began to evaporate as she watched the dark eyes grow colder by the minute.

"Did you want boiled coffee?" He asked. "I'm afraid that's what you'll be getting."

"Oh," she said, sidestepping both of them to get to the stove. She grabbed the pot just before the brown liquid oozed from the edge of the spout.

Robin, you're jinxed, she thought glumly, turning off the burner and taking the pot to the sink, then pouring herself a cup out of spite. When she tilted the cup and the thick mess entered her mouth, she had to bite her lips not to yelp at her scorched tongue.

Carefully, she placed the cup in the sink and glanced over her shoulder. Nobody was in sight; from the living room, she could hear the sound of Craig talking with his sons.

She poured out the dregs of the coffee, then rinsed the pot, and went in search of a teakettle. She finally located one on a bottom shelf, rinsed it out and filled it with fresh water. Then she headed back to her room to unpack her herbal tea bags.

Back in the kitchen, she put a tea bag in the cup and waited for the steam to rise from the kettle. Spotting a loaf of bread, she decided she could at least munch a piece of bread with her tea, since nothing else was offered.

She pulled out a slice of bread, then dropped the twistem on the floor as the kettle began to sing and she dashed over to retrieve it before anything else got burned.

At that precise moment Craig strolled back through the kitchen, looking for a wastebasket.

She tried to push a smile onto her face but never quite made it. Didn't seem to matter anyway, because his eyes flicked over her dismissively and landed on the dirty dishes in the sink. Then he leaned down to pick up the twistem from the bread wrapper.

"Thanks." She took it from him and retied the bread. "What can I fix for you?"

"Nothing." While his tone of voice was low and quiet, the look in his eyes said volumes. He was obviously irritated as he reached for the wastebasket and returned to the living room.

Robin placed one hand on her hip and arched her brow. No matter what she did, she seemed to be blundering at every turn, and his gruff responses were beginning to get on her nerves. Maybe this wasn't going to work after all.

The creak of the refrigerator door turned her attention to Will, hovering in the background. Taking a deep breath to calm herself, she focused on the little boy, who seemed so quiet and withdrawn, and the expression in his eyes was one she had not yet interpreted. She could sense sadness and loneliness and perhaps longing. For his mother? Or at least a friend.

"Will, what's your favorite food?" she asked pleasantly.

He stood, holding the milk, obviously considering her question.

"Hamburgers and french fries," he mumbled.

Ah, now that she could handle! "Hey, that's mine too. What do you say we have that for lunch? Provided you have the ingredients on hand."

Silently, he walked over to a bottom cabinet and lugged out a huge sack of potatoes. Then he returned to the refrigerator and opened the freezer compartment, pointing to several packages of ground beef.

"Great!" She gave him a big smile. "Now what time do you guys eat lunch?"

He shot a glance toward the living room, obviously wondering why she wasn't asking his dad about that. "I don't know. Depends on when Harley gets it ready."

"Eleven or twelve?"

He hesitated, still looking uncertain about what to say. "I guess so. But we won't be here. We're going to town."

"Oh."

A flush of embarrassment touched her cheeks. She was really messing up with this job.

"Then we'll have hamburgers and french fries for supper," she promised, speaking loud enough for Craig to hear.

If he heard, he gave no acknowledgment as he began to scold Zack about getting dressed. Trying to drown out his words, which were a reminder of how stern he could be, she pulled down a pound of ground beef. Staring at the pound of meat in her hand, she tried to calculate how much would be needed. She took the package to the counter, then hesitated. Was one package enough?

Squaring her shoulders, she forced herself to confront Craig just as he finished reprimanding Zack.

"Excuse me, but how many people will I be serving dinner to tonight? Are there ranch hands who—"

"Only Sam," he answered crisply. His attention was focused on Zack, who was down on his knees scooping spilled cereal from the floor and putting it in the wastebasket. "We're going into town so we won't be here for lunch." He laid several bills on the counter. "And if you want to drive in to the grocery and pick out what you need…"

Returning to the freezer, she saw there was plenty of meat, so she pulled out another package and placed it on the counter.

Locating a pencil and pad, she began to open and close cabinets, making out a grocery list. She'd show Mr. Craig Cameron a thing or two about her cooking.

Her thoughts moved on to long, lanky Sam, who had disappeared soon after her introduction. And where was this Harley, the former cook? she wondered. Kathy had said something about his being incapacitated, but now Robin suspected he had probably gotten enough of Craig Cameron's temper and hit the road in search of a more pleasant employer.

Those now-familiar boots were thudding her way again, but she kept to her task, ignoring his approach.

"The boys and I will finish chores," he said, "and then we're going to town. We'll be back around four. I keep a housekey under the back step, if you need it."

She looked up from the potatoes she was scrubbing. "Thanks." She watched him turn to leave, then added, "If the boys would rather stay here, I'll be glad to watch them."

He hesitated, meeting her eyes for the first time. Something flickered across his face, as swift as lightning, something she could only term as gentle, maybe even compassionate. It was the same expression she had seen on his face the night before when she burned her arm. She waited for him to speak, expecting him to say something…well, pleasant, at least.

But he looked away, shaking his head. "I'll take them with me." With that he turned and headed out the door, without so much as a thank-you.

You're welcome, she wanted to yell after him. Placing a hand on her hip, she stared after him for a moment as anger nudged her temper. Obviously, he had decided to put up with her for a week, endure whatever cooking she did, and then let her go.

But a week might be too long if his attitude didn't improve.

Seven

As soon as Craig and the boys drove off, Robin snatched up her shoulder bag and stuffed the grocery list and bills into it.

"Whoever heard of not having a phone," she fussed to herself, eager to call Kathy and burn her ears for sticking her with this grumpy man and his rowdy boys!

Sailing down the hall, she stopped to turn off the generator. All she needed now was to run the battery down. She had the feeling that they were all just waiting for her to make another wrong move, and it was precisely that challenge that was keeping her there.

Robin drove into Caribou Creek, searching for the local grocery. In front of the café, she could see the familiar white pickup, and she realized he had chosen to bring the boys to the café rather than subject them to another one of her meals. Honestly, how much more of this could she take?

Spotting a small grocery, she slammed on her brakes and wheeled into the parking space. She was going to stay on, just to show them she was as tough as they were.

Hopping out of the car, she hurried toward the grocery when she spotted a pay phone beside the front door. Changing direction, she charged toward the phone and dug into her purse for coins. Finding none, she decided to place a collect call to Kathy.

Once the operator finished her speech and a sleepy-sounding Kathy accepted the call, Robin let go.

"Thanks a lot for this job, cousin! You're a real pal."

"Oh, you're welcome," Kathy yawned, missing the satire. "So, are the eggs done yet?"

"Naturally," Robin shot back. "Along with the country ham and redeye gravy. Anything else?"

Kathy was awake and laughing now. "Wash your mouth out with soap for such a lie. Did you burn the toast?"

Robin winced at the memory of last night's disaster. Little did Kathy know how close she had come to hitting the mark.

"Touché. Well, I do appreciate the opportunity to be here. This is a beautiful ranch, Kathy. But you didn't tell me the guy was so—"

"Handsome? I wanted to surprise you."

Robin forced herself to lower her voice as an older couple walked by, and she turned her back so that she could speak more privately.

"Well, I've had more than one surprise. Kathy, how old did you tell him I was, for heaven's sake?"

"Let's just say I painted the picture of an old maid school-teacher who's a whiz in the kitchen."

"You what?" Robin gasped, and then suddenly the absurdity of the entire thing struck her as a bit funny. Kathy's laughter over the wire was contagious, and Robin began smiling in spite of herself.

"Just wait until I get my hands on you."

"Oh, I think you'd rather get your hands on him!"

"Will you stop it?" she laughed. Just then, she turned to see Zach behind her. Craig wasn't far behind. Her smile faded at his stern expression. "Hey, I gotta go."

"Okay, now watch your step," Kathy said, just before she hung up. Robin thought it was the most sensible thing she had said during the entire conversation.

Eight

❧

R obin was humming to herself as she sliced the potatoes. She knew how to slice potatoes in their skins, coat them with a special spice, then bake them. Everyone who tasted them usually raved. Rummaging around for a cookie sheet for baking the potatoes, she thought back to her antics with Zack.

She was beginning to feel pleased with herself about the meal. Maybe she was going to have some fun here, in spite of everyone's efforts to prevent it.

Robin reached for the pan of potatoes, trying to gauge the amount she was about to prepare. Should feed a small army, she decided, wandering over to the stove and testing the oven. It was good and hot, thanks to that searing gas flame, with which she was learning to cope.

Dumping the potatoes into a bowl of spicy seasoning to coat them, she thought of the Cameron guys. She was determined to prepare a meal that would please the worst critic—namely Craig Cameron.

As her eyes strayed to the sink and the window overhead, she watched his tall muscular body move at a swift pace toward the barn where Sam was hammering away on a fence post.

Absently, she reached over to pull the curtain back for a better look, and in doing so spotted the red skin below her wrist. She thought back to those minutes when a very gentle man had applied ointment and finished the cooking without a word of complaint.

Where had that man gone, she wondered? He hadn't even asked about her burn today. Obviously, he didn't care.

Shaking her head, she turned back to the potatoes. It was as though a mystery man had slipped into the kitchen last night, a man who seemed to possess a sweet, caring nature. But the man she had met on the road was the man who really lived here, the man who looked at her with nothing more than irritation and indifference.

Her dinner turned out to be a major success, with her hamburgers cooked just right and the baked french fries drawing praise from Sam and second helpings for Will and Craig. Zack had grabbed for a third handful before his father captured his arm and gently reminded him he would get a stomachache if he didn't slow down.

Sam had kept up a lively conversation about his fence repairing, and Craig had finally joined in with some enthusiasm. From the nature of the conversation, Robin gathered that major repairs were being made around the ranch.

"When we finish with the outbuildings, I may want to brace the porch a bit," Craig said, looking at Sam. "Depending on circumstances," he added, lapsing into silence.

"What circumstances, Dad?" Will asked, his eyes curious.

Craig looked across the table at Will, and for a moment Robin saw the love he felt for his sons, transparent in his eyes.

"Will, we have to go down to Seattle later on to visit your grandparents—"

"I don't wanna go!" Zack burst out. "Grandma fusses at me all the time."

Robin's eyes shot to Zack's face, and she sensed his frustration. Although his little face was flushed, a white line circled his mouth. He seemed really upset. Aware that Craig had glanced her way, checking her reaction, she grabbed the bowl of fruit.

"Will, would you like some canned peaches?"

Will's shoulders had slumped forward during the interchange between his father and brother. Distractedly, he looked toward the bowl, then Robin, and shook his head. As their eyes met, Robin saw in Will's dark eyes a sadness so deep and desperate that it wrenched her heart. Beside him, Craig had fallen silent and, to her surprise, was pushing back his plate.

"When are you gonna play that guitar?" Zack asked. He seemed to hop from one subject to another before anyone could catch up.

She arched a brow and decided not to mention the fact that he must have been prowling in her room. "Well, let's see."

Robin took a deep breath and followed her instincts. She had to do something for these boys, and she knew her time was limited. They needed so much, and she could give them so little. One thing she did know and could share was what they all seemed to need most.

"Mr. Cameron," she began, looking him squarely in the eye, "since tomorrow—"

"Why are you calling him Mister?" Zack interrupted her. "Sounds funny, you calling him Mister."

"That's right," Craig agreed matter-of-factly. "Please call me Craig. Zack, don't interrupt Miss Grayson when she's speaking." He looked back at Robin. "You were saying something about tomorrow."

Robin nodded, trying to pick up her train of thought. "Since tomorrow is Sunday, would it be okay if I got out my guitar and we sang some hymns out on the porch? I usually go to church and...well—" She faltered then, seeing in his eyes the same sadness that had been reflected in his son's face moments before.

"We used to go to church," Will said dully, staring at his glass of milk. All eyes turned to him for a moment, then Sam jumped in.

"Miss Grayson, that sure sounds like a good idea. Lucille's daughter is visiting from Golden, and, well..." He glanced cautiously toward Craig. "I kind of thought I'd bring them out to see the ranch, if Mr. Cameron doesn't object."

Robin looked back at Craig, relieved to see that his expression had softened. "Sure, Sam. Bring your friends out. We like to have company, don't we, guys?"

The boys nodded, and Sam grinned from ear to ear as he looked back at Robin. "Lucille lives in Skookumchuk, where I'm from. We been seeing each other for the past year, ever since her divorce."

Robin nodded and smiled, wondering how she was supposed to respond to that statement. "I look forward to meeting your friend and her daughter," she said with a smile.

The grin spread to his ears. "She'd like to meet you. She loves guitar music."

Robin studied Sam for a moment, wondering about him. Every time she looked at him, she found herself thinking of Ichabod Crane. His clothes looked to be an extra large size, and still his bony wrists dangled at least an inch beyond his cuffs. His face was all bones and hollows, and his medium brown hair was graying just above his ears. Yet his blue eyes seemed to mirror a good heart, and he looked at Zack and Will with honest affection.

"I thought you were going to make cookies," Zack spoke up, having grabbed more french fries. Ketchup dribbled from his lips as he spoke.

"Zack, wipe your chin, please," his father quietly admonished.

"I'll make cookies tomorrow," Robin promised. Her eyes shot to Craig. "That is, if your father doesn't object to you having sweets." She had noticed Zack was pretty hyper; maybe sugar wasn't such a good idea, after all.

Craig's eyes lingered on her for a moment, then drifted to first Zack and then Will. "Cookies would be a nice treat for the boys. What do you think, Will?"

"I guess so," Will said quietly.

Robin nodded, thinking that more went with home-baked cookies than just the sugar; they all needed a little love thrown in. Especially their unpredictable father, she thought, as Sam stood up, pushing his chair back under the table.

"Well, I'd better be headin' in to see Lucille. Thanks, again, Miss Grayson."

"Just call me Robin," she smiled at him. "And that goes for you guys," she smiled at Will and Zack.

"Boys, take your plates to the sink," Craig instructed, "then I want you to go with me down to the barn. We need to straighten up the tack room."

"Daaaad!" Zack protested, then fell silent as his father glanced back at him.

"We had a deal, remember? More games for a little more work. It was even your idea, Zack." Craig turned toward Robin. "Thank you for dinner."

Turning his lips downward but saying nothing more, Zack dragged himself out of the chair. As much as he had eaten, Robin thought he needed to do laps around the yard.

"Boys—" Craig was looking from Zack to Will.

"I enjoyed my meal," Will said politely.

"Me, too," Zack said, and slowly a grin touched his mouth and lit the fire in his blue eyes.

"Thanks, I'm glad," Robin smiled back.

As the three headed out the back door in the growing twilight, Robin's thoughts lingered on Craig. She appreciated the sincere note in his voice when he complimented her on the meal and prompted the boys to do so. Her heart kept telling her he was a kind and caring person, yet he was abrupt, unpredictable, almost harsh at times.

While they were out of the house, Robin mixed up a double batch of oatmeal cookies and put the dough in the refrigerator for use the next day. Then she wandered out to the porch, staring across the valley as the soft gray twilight began to fade.

She dropped into a porch rocker, and her eyes followed the stream in its winding path toward the upper end of the valley. She couldn't wait to hike back to the cabin when she had a few hours to herself. She kept thinking about the verses underscored in Jenny Russell's Bible, and she could imagine a woman in a crude cabin up that valley somewhere, enduring droughts and blizzards.

Still Jenny Russell had been happy, Granny had told her. She was with the man she loved and a daughter she adored and life was good. Until Skook, her adventurous husband, died at the age of thirty-nine.

The sadness Jenny Russell must have felt brought a sigh to Robin's lips. She had always felt a longing she didn't quite understand when she heard about Skook and Jenny Russell and the land they had named Sundance.

Squinting through the sunlight, Robin thought how odd it was to be sitting on this porch all alone in the twilight, looking at the land that she had wanted to see for years. After reading that verse in the Bible the previous night, she had felt a peace, a sense of belonging. She thought about the verse that had sustained Jenny Russell. That verse was appropriate for her as well, in her dealings with Craig Cameron and Zack and Will.

Their voices drifted up from the barn, and she felt a deep sense of contentment. She was glad she hadn't followed that first temptation to throw down her apron and quit that morning. She only hoped she could last until she had a chance to go exploring.

Glancing back toward the barn, she saw Will coming up the path to the house. She so wanted to make friends with him, but he seemed to have built a wall around his little heart, afraid to let himself care for someone.

"Hey, Will," she called pleasantly, "did you guys get your work done?"

"I got mine finished," he said as he reached the steps and lingered. "It didn't take me long."

She decided to try an approach that sometimes worked with her students. "Do you have any hobbies, Will?"

He nodded solemnly. "I collect arrowheads."

"Oh, you do? I would love to see your collection—if you wouldn't mind showing me, I mean."

He dashed up the steps and went into the house. She drew another rocker closer to hers. In a few moments he was back, holding a shoebox in his hand.

"I picked these up around the ranch," he said shyly, glancing at the empty rocker beside her but choosing not to sit down.

"Oh, Will, those are nice," Robin said, staring down at the varied assortment of arrowheads; varing from one-half inch wide to one-and-a-half inches long.

"Dad said these small ones were probably used to kill birds and small game. But this one," he said lifting a large, perfectly shaped obsidian arrowhead, "was for big game."

"Wow. Let me see that," she said, carefully picking up the large arrowhead with razor-sharp sides.

"I measured it," Will said. "It's four and a half inches long and three and one-fourth inches wide."

"Yeah, that's really something."

"Harley said it probably belonged to a famous chief."

Robin nodded. "You know, Will, this could have come from Anaheim Peak, a famous obsidian mountain near Anaheim Lake."

"Where is Anaheim Lake? Can we go there?"

"I've never been there, but it's between Williams Lake and Bella Coola."

"I betcha Harley's been there. Maybe we could all go out there and get some obsidian and make our own arrowheads."

She smiled. "That would be fun. Did your dad tell you much about the Indians here?"

"Not much." He sat down in the rocker.

"Well, my parents were teachers, and Dad's great passion was history. He talked a lot about the Indians. According to the early journals, the Kootenay Indians settled this part of the country. That's why the main river that runs through this valley is named the Kootenay."

"I'd like to have been an explorer," Will said quietly, staring off into space.

"Me, too," she said, pleased to find a common interest with Will. "History was my favorite subject in school, and Dad and I used to pore over his journals. He collected old history books the way you collect arrowheads."

Will turned and looked at her, his dark eyes shining. He was clearly taken by this conversation.

"I remember Dad liked to talk about David Thompson," she said. "Do you know who he was?"

Will nodded. "An explorer."

"Right, and a trapper and surveyor as well. He worked for the Hudson Bay Company, but he'd had a yearning to cross those Rockies and see what was on this side of the mountains. He came into British Columbia in...," she faltered. "I remember, it was the early 1800s."

"We have a book about Canada. I'll get it." Will leapt out of the rocker.

Robin lifted a brow, watching him zip through the door. At least she had hit on a subject that interested him. That was great. And it was refreshing to see someone his age so interested in history.

He was back in a flash, a thick book cradled in his arms. He extended it proudly to her. She could see it was not a school text, but rather a personal copy.

"That's Dad's book."

She nodded, looking at a nice edition of Thompson's travels.

"Great." She opened the book and found a map. "See, I can show you the route Thompson took." She placed her thumbnail on the site of Hudson Bay's York Factory. "He left with some other men and came up the Nelson River here..."

She traced the route with her finger, ending up at the Rocky Mountains.

"They crossed over what is now Howes Pass and dropped in on the Columbia River, see? Of course they had an Indian guide showing them which way to go. They came up the river to Columbia Lake, and from there it's only about a mile overland to the Kootenay. Look at this, Will, the Columbia River is running north, and here's the Kootenay River running south."

"Neat," Will grinned, looking up at her. His dark eyes held something that had not been there before, a look of...admiration, maybe? As she looked into his shining eyes, she could almost see his father reflected back. They were so alike, and it was strange sitting so close to Will, enjoying a conversation and glimpsing the little boy Craig must have been.

"Well," she sighed, closing the book, "I got way off the subject, didn't I? We were talking about arrowheads, and suddenly I jumped into rivers."

His grin broadened into a smile as he looked from her back

to his box of arrowheads. "Dad says these probably came from the Kootenay Indians."

"Yeah, they probably did. Do you go out looking for arrowheads much? I like to do that kind of thing. My sisters never cared anything about it though, or Mom either. Dad was usually busy."

Will stared at her, chewing his lip. She waited for him to suggest they go together sometime, but since he didn't, she decided to drop the subject.

Zack came flying up the trail at that moment, yelling to Will. "Dad says we need you, Will. You ran out!" Dirt streaks ran down Zack's face, and his clothes were filthy.

"I did not. I was through and—" He hesitated, glancing at Robin. "Well, okay. I guess if he really wants me to…" He got up and took his shoebox back inside.

Watching them argue their way back to the barn, Robin smiled to herself, thinking about the boys and their father. Then, glancing at the book in her lap, she closed the cover. She was getting too involved here, and she couldn't let that happen. She was only here for a short time, and then she was leaving. In the meantime, she had better back off. After all, she could lose her heart to the boys as well as the man.

She got up and went inside, leaving the book on a table. An ache slipped through her bones, reminding her that she was exhausted from the long day. It was not yet nine, but she knew her employer would be relieved if he returned to the house and discovered that she had already gone to bed. That way, there wouldn't be that awkwardness that seemed to hang between them each time they were in the same room together.

Thinking she would read for a while, she snuggled down under the comforter, but sleep lay heavy on her lids. She was barely able to close the Bible and turn off the light before sleep claimed her. And again she forgot to set an alarm.

At first it was just a vague irritation, then from the depths of her sleep she became aware of a slight nudging. On her shoulder. She was curled on her side, her red head buried in the soft pillow, her muscles completely relaxed. But that nudging grew stronger, bringing first a frown nestled between her eyebrows, then slowly one eye dragged open.

What time was it?

The morning sunlight drifted through the cracked drapes, and she realized with a start she had overslept again. But what was it that had awakened her? Something moved behind her. Someone was in bed with her!

Her head rolled on the pillow. Suddenly she was staring at the most grotesque face she had ever seen in her life. A scream ripped from her throat and hit the rafters, shrill and desperate.

Nine

❧

The face drew back along with the small body that toppled onto the floor. At that moment, Craig Cameron rushed to the open door and shot an anxious look in Robin's direction.

"What?"

Robin heard a movement underneath her, like an animal burrowing its way through a tunnel. Only the tunnel was under her bed and the...*thing* that had been lying beside her was now thudding around beneath her.

She bolted upright, drawing the covers up to her chin, unable to speak. Her throat felt raw from the blood-curdling scream that had drawn Will to the doorway, as well.

"It's Zack with his mask," Will said, looking up at his father.

Suddenly the movement under her bed ceased. Robin raked through her mussed hair and thought about that hideous thing that had awakened her. That awful concoction of warts and bloody teeth that greeted her had indeed been a mask.

Craig sprang into action, striding toward the bed and kneeling down to yank up the dust ruffle.

"Zack, get out from under the bed this minute!" Craig was obviously angry, yet he had not raised his voice.

Suddenly, Zack popped out from under the bed, his blond hair awry, a bulge extending from underneath his pajama shirt.

Robin leaned forward and caught a glimpse of something gray and ugly before he backed against the wall. She heaved a sigh, recalling all the pranks she had played on her sisters. And the punishment that followed.

"To your room, young man!" Craig ordered, a broad hand yanking Zack's arm. "You can forget that trip to Billy Anderson's house next week."

Zack dug his heels in and looked at his father with stricken eyes. "Billy's got a new pony!"

Robin could see that he was fighting back the tears, and she felt that familiar tug at her heartstrings once again.

"Wait," she said gently. "I don't want to interfere, but if you punish him, then I won't get to."

All eyes turned to her, each face registering a different element of surprise.

"What I mean is, I'm already thinking of something to do to him," she wrinkled her nose at Zack, "so if you don't mind, let's just leave this little incident between Zack and me!"

"He gets away with murder," Will grumbled, trudging off.

"No, he doesn't," Craig called after Will.

"I'll get you back, Zack," she said, shaking a finger at him in a teasing manner. "Now if you gentlemen will excuse me, I think I'll get dressed."

Craig waited a moment, then said, "Zack, I believe you owe her an apology, at the very least."

A lopsided grin tilted Zack's lips as he looked at Robin with new respect.

"I'm sorry," he said, slowly and deliberately. Then he tilted back his blond head to examine his father's expression. "Now can I go to Billy's?"

"Depends on how you behave until then," Craig responded, letting go of his arm.

Robin suspected from Craig's milder tone of voice that Craig was relieved not to have to punish his son. Zack scrambled from the room, as though fearful his father might change his mind.

Craig hesitated, propping a broad shoulder against the door frame. "Thanks," he said, his eyes meeting hers. "That was nice of you."

Her eyes locked with his, and suddenly she was aware of her heart racing in a strange way—just as it had when he'd swabbed ointment on her burned skin and looked at her with concern. She moistened her dry lips while absently running a hand through her hair to smooth it in place.

"Zack just has an adventurous spirit, and I can relate to him," Robin replied.

"I'm beginning to see that," he said with a grin.

Craig was coming to realize that she was not at all the shallow redhead he had judged her to be when he met her on the road Friday. His experience with women was limited. He and Brenda had married right out of high school, and it occurred to him that he tended to compare all women to Brenda and that that might be unfair to others.

He recalled Robin's conversation on the pay phone, the one Zack had interrupted. She had been laughing with someone over the phone in town, and he had automatically assumed she had called Kathy and the joke was on him. Maybe not. Even so, what did it really matter if she was kind to the boys? They both needed kindness in their lives now; they desperately needed that.

"I can relate to using a mask on occasions other than Halloween," Robin spoke again. "I've done it myself," she said with a mischievous grin.

Her employer continued to stare at her. What was he thinking? Whatever it was, the dark eyes were soft and warm before he stepped back into the hall, closing her door softly.

She took a deep breath, trying to steady her ragged heart. Swinging her legs onto the floor, she groped for her tennis shoes. It was wearing on her nerves to try and carry on a conversation with this man when he spoke in a soft voice. His eyes were pools of mystery. He was an adventure she must never allow herself to explore. And yet she was still thinking of him as she hopped from the bed and rushed to the closet to get her clothes.

Stop this, she told herself. *This can't work. This is ridiculous.* She hurried to the dresser and began to brush her hair. As she stared at her reflection, she saw in her eyes a strange new sparkle. She knew it had something to do with Craig Cameron. And that scared her. She called up in her memory that seventeenth summer when Ross, the cowboy in Calgary, had ridden off with her heart.

By the time she dressed and headed for the kitchen, Craig and the boys were out in the yard, talking to a plump, gray-haired gentleman who spoke loud enough to be heard from one side of the valley to the other.

"The grandkids are coming for a visit today. They'll probably run us ragged. Still, we're glad to have Myra home again, even if it's a divorce that brought her. Jack's kids live with us, too,

76

you know, and they came in from town with a box of video games last night. Thought you boys might wanna come over tomorrow afternoon, play games, and meet the rest of the clan."

Robin wasn't exactly eavesdropping, but the back door was open, and out of curiosity she found herself wandering to the window.

"Myra will probably bake up one of her good cakes tomorrow," he said, looking squarely at Craig. "So you guys come on over around four, and I'll lay some steaks on the grill."

Zack was practically jumping up and down, and even Will, usually reticent, looked pleased by the invitation.

"Thanks, Mr. Walton," Craig said. "The boys would enjoy that, but hold off on my steak. I'm not sure I can stay."

"I imagine you need a little fun, too," Walton replied, elbowing Craig as though a private joke had passed between them. "Where's Harley?" he glanced toward the house.

"Haven't you heard? Harley broke his leg rodeoing."

The older man shook his head. "More likely he broke it trying to clog with Hazel Wallace at one of those newfangled saloons." He turned back to his green pickup. "Well, see you guys tomorrow." He climbed in and slammed the door.

"All right, Mr. Walton." Craig smiled. "Thanks for the invitation."

"How many times I gotta tell you to drop that *mister* stuff?" The man's hand shot out of the truck, slapping Craig on the shoulder.

Robin turned back to the herb tea she was making. Maybe Craig was too preoccupied to pick up on the situation, but she suspected Mr. Walton might be playing Cupid for the benefit of his daughter. In a way, it was amusing, or would be to some people, but she didn't particularly like the idea.

Over oatmeal and whole wheat toast, Zack kept up a lively

chatter. He was excited about the video games and their invitation on Monday. At one point, Robin felt Will's eyes on her, studying her quietly. Strange how he reminded her so much of his father at times, particularly his eyes.

"Are you coming with us?" Will asked quietly, looking at Robin.

She cleared her throat. "No, Will, I need to catch up on some things here," she responded, reaching for a new jar of honey.

"Like what?" Zack demanded.

"Zack, it's rude to be so nosy," his father scolded.

"Actually, I'm making a Halloween mask!"

Her reply brought a snicker from Zack, who seemed delighted by the prospect of another game. Even Will gave a little smile, while Craig merely studied her with that odd expression that she hadn't quite analyzed.

"You gonna surprise me?" Zack asked, his blue eyes sparkling.

"I just might." She matched his mischievous grin. "So you better stay on your toes."

Even Craig was smiling, and the rest of the meal was pleasant, with Craig and the boys pitching in to put away the food and take dishes to the sink. Craig lingered, pointing out where everything was located, although she had long since learned.

"Thanks, and now I'll be just fine on my own in here," she said gently, lining up the dishes and reaching for the detergent.

"Don't forget to wrap the bread up," Craig said, still hanging around. "When the air is dry—"

"I know!" She bit her tongue, wishing she hadn't snapped. She felt she was quite capable of running the kitchen. Still, Craig continued to remind her of mundane things like wrapping the bread or putting the milk in the refrigerator or wiping the traces of honey from the jar.

"Look." She turned to face him and tried to speak calmly. "I know you're accustomed to doing things here, but please allow me to earn my board and keep. I've lived in Canada most of my life, and I know the air is dry—"

"More dry here than—"

"And I know that nobody wants their fingers sticking to a jar of honey, so if you don't mind—"

"Excuse me! I didn't mean to offend you," he snapped back.

With her arms plunged in dishes and soapsuds, she glared at him. Standing in the center of the kitchen, his hands on his hips, he glared back.

Suddenly Robin wondered if all this was about kitchen things or if they were both feeling a tension build that had nothing to do with food. She took a deep breath, looking down at the soap bubble on her arm. "You didn't," she said softly. "I just wanted to let you know that I'd prefer to handle things on my own."

As soon as she spoke those words, she knew she had put her foot in her mouth. She caught her breath, waiting for him to remind her about the skillet of grease or make some reference to her burned arm.

To her relief, he merely turned and walked out of the kitchen without saying anything uncomplimentary. Or complimentary.

Why did she care? she wondered, feeling the tension mount at the base of her neck. "I *don't* care," she mumbled to herself. And she would try very hard to believe that.

Ten

Robin and the boys had just settled down on the porch to have their Sunday morning songfest. Craig had found an excuse to linger at the barn, and Robin had entertained the boys for half an hour, strumming chords on the guitar.

She had finally given up on anyone joining them and launched into "Jesus Loves Me" for Will and Zack, asking them to pretend they were in Sunday school. To her surprise, both began to sing with her, obviously familiar with the hymn.

As they sang, she recalled that one of the boys, or perhaps it was Craig, had said that their mother had taken them to Sunday school when they lived in Omak. Robin had not pursued the subject, fearing it might make the boys sad. Just as they launched into the second verse, Sam's pickup roared up the drive with Sam at the wheel and two other passengers inside.

"There's Sam and his girlfriend," Will observed quietly. He had slowly begun to enter into conversation, to Robin's relief.

A woman with bleached blond hair and a wide red smile sat beside him. A girl huddled against the door, looking out of sorts, perhaps even angry.

Robin waved as the truck ground to a halt and Sam unfolded

his long frame from behind the wheel.

"Ain't it a pretty morning?" he yelled.

"Yes, it is," Robin replied. Like Will and Zack, she found herself curious about their guests. The girl came out of the truck, brushing her clothes as though Sam's truck were a hay wagon. Her mother was a bit plump, yet attractive, in jeans and a T-shirt that advertised a national park. The girl's T-shirt blazed with a colorful rock band.

"Good morning," Robin smiled at the woman.

"Hi." She rushed forward, extending a hand with inches of red acrylic nails. "I'm Lucille."

"I"m Robin." Her eyes drifted back to the girl who kept her distance, surveying everyone with narrowed eyes.

"This is my daughter, Kelsey," Lucille motioned the girl forward. "Come on up, honey, and meet these folks."

Looking as though she might be facing a barnyard of manure, Kelsey slowly picked her way toward the porch, glancing from Zack to Will, then letting her eyes linger curiously on Robin.

"Hi, Kelsey, I'm Robin."

"Hi." Her voice was flat and cold.

As Robin looked at the girl, judging her to be around sixteen, she noticed her eyes were a pretty green; however, the blue eyeshadow and thick mascara were not calculated to complement Kelsey's eyes. Short brown hair framed small features, and her figure was trim in the jeans and T-shirt. In another year she would probably develop into a very pretty girl if her makeup and her attitude were adjusted.

"We're singing 'Jesus Loves Me,'" Zack stated proudly.

At that, Kelsey's pouty lips curved into a little smirk.

"Mind if we sit here on the porch steps and listen to the music?" Sam asked, laying a long arm around Lucille's shoulder.

"Not if you sing along," Robin said, strumming a few chords

and pretending not to notice the way Kelsey remained aloof. The teen seemed to dig her new leather boots deeper in the dirt, determined not to come near the porch.

At that moment Craig walked up from the barn, nodding to Lucille and Kelsey while Sam gushed through the introductions. Sam was proud of his girlfriend; Robin could see that. Kelsey, however, appeared to present a major problem for the couple. There was a look of open hostility on her face when her eyes moved from her mother to Sam.

"Let's sing another song," Zack insisted loudly.

"Okay. Lucille, is there anything in particular you like?"

The question took the older woman by surprise. "Well," she glanced uncertainly at Sam, "if you're singing hymns, my mother's favorite was 'The Old Rugged Cross.'"

"I know that one," Robin nodded. "Mom likes it, too."

Glancing at the boys, she saw both faces had grown pale, and she suspected they were thinking of their mother. She bit her lip, wishing she could have spared them that sadness as she forced herself to plunge into the hymn, an older one which they might not have heard.

"On a hill far away stood an old rugged cross,
The emblem of suffering and shame;
And I love that old cross where the dearest and best
For a world of lost sinners was slain..."

As she sang, Robin's eyes drifted over the group. Zack was mouthing a word here and there, Will was trying, and Craig was humming softly in the background. Sam looked as though he had never heard the song, while huge tears were forming in Lucille's eyes. Kelsey had turned her head in the direction of the pasture, watching the horses graze.

"So I'll cherish the old rugged cross,
Till my trophies at last I lay down,

I will cling to the old rugged cross,
And exchange it someday for a crown."

As Robin's lilting soprano voice filled the sunlit morning and she struck the last chord, the group became silent. Then Lucille began to sniff. Sam hugged her against him, looking as though he too might shed a tear.

"Mother died last year," Lucille's voice wobbled, "and—"

Muttering a curse, Kelsey whirled and ran across the yard to the pasture that enclosed the horses.

"What's wrong with—?"

Robin put a hand on Zack's arm, shaking her head, to stop his question. He swallowed the last word as everyone's eyes followed Kelsey to the fence, where she stood with her back to them, looking out at the horses.

"She hates for me to get emotional," Lucille said, taking the handkerchief Sam offered. "But this last year has been so rotten..." Lucille looked from Sam to Robin.

Robin nodded sympathetically.

"I made some mistakes," Lucille said, looking down at the handkerchief and wringing it between her fingers, "and nobody will let me forget them. Except Sam," she said, turning worshipful eyes to him. "Sam's the only one who believes in me, except maybe..." She hesitated, looking back at Robin. She swallowed as another wash of tears came to her eyes. "Except maybe that person you sang about who died on a cross."

Robin nodded. "That's right. Nothing's too difficult for him to handle."

Nobody responded to that, not even Zack, although the boys stared wide-eyed at her. She suspected their minds were filled with thoughts about their own lives and the loss of their mother. Craig, seated on the corner of the porch, looked across at Robin with an expression of sadness and pain and something more. Grief, she decided, looking away. So much pain resided in one family—and so much need for the healing love of the one she had sung about. Everyone here seemed to be in need of that love and forgiveness.

Her eyes moved toward the girl who stood apart from them, seeming more alone than anyone. And more desperate.

She laid down her guitar and stood. "Maybe I'll go down and get acquainted with Kelsey."

Lucille was blowing her nose and trying to regain her composure while Zack was muttering something. One word was quite audible: "Brat."

As Robin walked away from the group, she heard Craig clearing his throat, and she hoped he wasn't about to scold Zack for merely being honest. On the contrary, he was inviting Sam to show Lucille around the ranch; he even suggested everyone might go horseback riding later on.

"Kelsey would love that!" Lucille exclaimed.

Robin watched the girl's back stiffen at the sound of her mother's voice, quite distinct even from forty yards away.

"Hi." Robin reached Kelsey's side and propped her arms on the fence, just as Kelsey was doing.

Kelsey whirled on her. "Do you believe that?" Her green eyes fired the challenge like a bullet.

"Believe—" Was this about going horseback riding or did the question pertain to her mother?

"That some man died on a cross for everybody's sins," Kelsey taunted, her voice as hard as the nails in the fence post.

"Sure I do. If I didn't believe it, I wouldn't be singing about it. Why are you so sure he didn't?"

"I didn't say that," she replied crossly, staring out at the horses. "It's just that I'm tired of all that…"

She lapsed into more expletives until Robin touched her arm.

84

"Hold it. I don't need to hear that kind of language to get your point. Nor do those little boys," she inclined her head toward the porch.

Kelsey shrugged her arm away and glared into the distance.

"Kelsey, why don't you try and have a good time? You just might, you know, if you give us a chance."

Kelsey said nothing. She just kept staring at the horses.

"Do you like to ride?" Robin decided to try another approach.

The girl shrugged lightly. "Maybe. I never get to, though. I live with my old man and his new wife, and all they do is watch television and drink beer."

Robin glanced back at Lucille, who had finally composed herself and was giggling at something Sam had said. "You live with your dad through the week and see your mom on weekends?"

Kelsey nodded. "Yeah, I'd rather be in Skookumchuk where my friends are, but Dad got me in the divorce." She turned to Robin, speaking slowly, hoping to shock her. "My mom was sleeping around."

Robin didn't bat an eye. "I'm not going to judge your mom, Kelsey. Or your dad or even you. I just asked if you'd like to go riding with us. Seems to me you're due for some fun."

The hard green eyes began to soften as Kelsey took a long breath and darted a glance back at the people on the porch.

"Do I have to hang around them?" she asked.

"By them, are you referring to the boys or to your mom and Sam?"

"I don't mind the boys," she said, her eyes sweeping Zack and Will, and thereby answering Robin's question.

"Great. Zack and Will need a friend. Their mother died two years ago," she said, watching Kelsey's face.

Without saying so, she had reminded the girl that she still

had a mother who obviously regretted her mistakes and wanted desperately to patch up their relationship.

"That's tough—" She caught herself before another cuss word fell from her tongue. "Luck."

"Yes, it is. Want to help me dish out the spaghetti?"

She shrugged. "Might as well. But I don't like spaghetti," she added, tagging after Robin.

Eleven

❧

R obin decided to serve the lunch buffet style, thinking she needed to keep the mood relaxed and casual. She had asked Kelsey to help with the buffet, and the girl had shown remarkable ingenuity by locating wicker baskets and using them, rather than dishes, as serving pieces. She had lined the baskets with napkins for bread and chips and even dashed out the back door to grab a handful of wildflowers to stick in a glass in the center of the table.

"Mom taught me that," she admitted, as she added the final touch.

"Great," Robin smiled, working quickly with the lunch. Soon after breakfast she had browned two packages of ground beef, made a spicy sauce, and boiled the noodles. Then she had combined the cooked noodles and the sauce in a huge Pyrex dish and grated cheese on top. The dish was waiting for her now; all that remained was placing it in the oven long enough for it to heat through.

Craig strolled into the kitchen, peering into the oven. "Did you put that thing in all by yourself?" he asked Robin.

She looked surprised. "Of course."

"Isn't your arm still a bit sore?"

It was, but Robin didn't want to admit it. She had prepared lunch on a surge of adrenaline with her arm sending up only a few vague complaints throughout the morning.

"I'm just fine," she called over her shoulder.

"Probably wouldn't admit it if you weren't," he said, almost under his breath.

"I probably wouldn't," she fired back, giving him a smile to show that she spoke in fun.

"Can I do anything to help?" he asked, which brought a curious glance from Kelsey.

"Nope, we've got it covered."

He sauntered back out, with Kelsey's eyes following him curiously.

"You two live together?" she whispered to Robin.

Trying again to maintain her poise with this outspoken girl, Robin reached for the potholders and shook her head. "Nope. I work here as a temporary cook while their regular mends from a broken leg."

"Sure," Kelsey said with a smirk.

"Hey, I'm telling you the truth. And if you don't believe I can earn a living as a cook, wait until you taste this spaghetti you don't like!"

Later, after everyone had taken their plates to the front porch or the kitchen table, whichever they preferred, Robin bumped into Kelsey at the buffet counter. She had just dipped the serving spoon into the spaghetti for the second time.

"Hey," Robin nudged her, "you don't like that stuff, remember?"

"And you said you were a good cook, remember?"

They laughed together, and as Robin glanced across the

room, she met Lucille's startled eyes. Apparently, the sight of her daughter laughing was a rarity these days.

After lunch, Lucille insisted on helping with the dishes while Kelsey tagged after Will and Zack to watch Craig and Sam saddle the horses.

"I can't tell you how much I appreciate you being so nice to Kelsey," Lucille began as soon as her daughter was out of earshot.

"Not a problem. She's a lovely girl."

Lucille stared at Robin for a moment, as though trying to be certain she had heard correctly. Then a smile of pride touched her red lips. "She is, isn't she? But I worry about her all the time."

Robin glanced at the woman, who was several inches shorter than she and several pounds heavier. Robin thought Lucille would be more attractive with less backcombing in her blond hair and a more subtle shade of lipstick. Nevertheless, she had noticed Sam looking at her with glowing approval. She smiled, turning back to Lucille.

"Just give her time and patience," Robin replied. "And lots of love. Things will work out."

"If only I could get custody of her again," Lucille sighed, lifting the cup towel to dry a plate. "You know, I'd give anything in the world to go back and undo my mistakes, but of course I can't." She sighed. "My ex-husband and I never got along. When he came home from work, all he wanted to do was melt into that recliner and bark orders. He never seemed to appreciate me, and even after I'd put in a ten-hour shift at the café, he never lifted his hand to help around the house."

She laid the plate down, then picked up another one to dry.

"Forest—that's the guy who owns the diner—had lost his wife to cancer the year before. He was lonely and kind and, well…" Her voice drifted off, but Robin could fill in the rest on her own.

"But you seem to be happy with Sam now," Robin replied.

"Oh, I am! Sam is wonderful to me. It's just that I miss having Kelsey and she—" Her eyes dropped to the plate again. "She has no respect for me. She was always a daddy's girl. She wanted to live with him instead of me because she thought he'd go on petting and pampering her. But then he got married and all that has changed. Now I guess she doesn't like either one of us much."

Robin didn't know how to respond to that, for obviously the girl had her problems, yet she suspected many of those problems stemmed from insecurity. She had seen others try to bluff their way through situations when they were crying on the inside.

The back door opened, and Craig stepped in. His eyes moved quickly from Lucille to Robin, and this time Robin saw something warm and kind in those eyes.

"Are you ladies almost finished?" he asked pleasantly. "We have the horses saddled up; in fact, the boys and Kelsey are already riding. Sam's with them, of course."

"Oh, I'm not much with horses, Mr. Cameron," Lucille said, dipping her eyes self-consciously. "If you don't mind, I'd rather just sit out on the porch and enjoy the view."

He nodded at that. "Okay. What about you, Robin?"

It was the first time he had spoken her name, and Robin was pleased that he wasn't being so formal with her.

"I'd love to, but I'll take a rain check and sit on the porch with Lucille."

His eyes lingered on her for a moment. "You sure? Will says you told him you've always been nuts about horses."

"Go on," Lucille urged. "You don't have to entertain me."

While there was nothing Robin would rather do than go horseback riding, she felt she should stay with Lucille. Maybe there would be another opportunity to ride.

"I'll take a rain check," she repeated, glancing back at Craig.

Their eyes locked for a moment, and neither seemed conscious of Lucille, who was making an attempt to slip quietly out of the kitchen. Then she accidentally bumped a chair, and Craig cleared his throat.

"So you get a rain check," he promised. And this time he smiled at her.

Robin felt as though she had seen that other man emerge again. The smile completely transformed his face, putting a glow in the dark eyes, softening the grim mouth, even accenting a dimple hidden deep in his cheek. His hair was neatly combed, and he wore a deep blue denim shirt and jeans. With broad shoulders and long legs, he towered over her, looking at her with that same expression of kindness that she had found the night she burned her arm.

Robin tried to drag her eyes away from him as all the warning signals started going off in her brain. But she stood there, mesmerized, aware in the depths of her soul that she was falling for Craig Cameron. And she was falling hard.

That knowledge forced her to decline again late in the afternoon after Sam, Lucille, and Kelsey had said their good-byes. Everyone seemed happy, and Kelsey had promised Robin she would come again. Zack and Will were playing tag in a far corner of the yard.

Robin lingered on the porch, resting comfortably in the wooden rocker, staring up the valley.

"Ready for a ride?" Craig asked as he walked around the corner of the house.

"I'm too comfortable just sitting here," she said with a sigh.

"You're probably exhausted. I'm afraid you got more than you bargained for today, not only as cook but psychologist, as well."

"I hope you don't think I was being too—"

He put up his hand to stop her. "Not at all. It was obvious to everyone that Kelsey left her bad attitude out in the yard by lunchtime. You're very good with kids," he said, his lower lip thrust between his teeth as he studied her thoughtfully.

She shrugged, looking away. "Well, I guess it's in my genes. My parents were both schoolteachers, and they often talked about their students. Most of the time, if there was a problem, they tried to speak privately, but I couldn't help hearing since our house was small. And I'm a teacher, too," she added, as an afterthought.

"What grade do you teach?" It was the first time he had asked her anything about herself.

Robin suspected he had warned himself to keep this arrangement as formal as possible, which meant limiting conversation to food or the boys.

"I've taught third grade the past two years," she answered, "but I prefer first grade, or even kindergarten. There's nothing quite as rewarding to me as the spark of learning that pops into a child's eye and the satisfaction of helping to open the doors of education to that child."

He stared at her, saying nothing. Beneath the heat of those dark eyes, she began to fidget.

"So Zack's going into second and Will's going into fourth at Wassa?"

Craig hesitated, brushing something from the leg of his jeans. "Zack's birthday is in August, so he's actually some months younger than many of his classmates, while Will's birthday is in April."

Robin nodded, trying to think what was unanswered. She couldn't quite define what he had avoided. Did it have something to do with the school they were attending or did it pertain to their ages? She prided herself on being intuitive, and she knew there was something behind his words.

"They both seem very bright," she said, trying to get at whatever had brought that brooding frown back to his face. She wanted to lift a hand, smooth the rumpled space between his dark brows. He seemed so troubled most of the time.

"Will does well in school. Zack could, I suppose, if only he would apply himself."

"Zack's grades aren't as good as you would like?"

He shook his head. "To tell you the truth, he barely passed first grade. His teacher kept complaining that he wouldn't pay attention, that he wasn't interested, that he disrupted the class. As you can imagine, there were several conferences, and one with the principal." He sighed. "Losing their mother made it more difficult, of course…"

"Of course," she responded gently. "You seem to have done a remarkable job with them. I can't begin to imagine all you've been through, but it's obvious that you love them very much. And that's the most important thing in rearing children."

He gazed at her and the frown began to disappear. "It's good to hear you say that. I do love them, and I'd do anything in the world for them." He turned and looked out across the valley, saying nothing more.

Watching him, Robin felt her heart going out to this man and his boys. She wanted to help Zack and Will, but she didn't want to interfere. Sometimes she felt a strong rapport with Craig, like right now. At other times he seemed so remote, and she sensed that he worked at keeping his distance from everyone. Especially her.

She cleared her throat. "While I'm here, I don't mind working with Zack a bit; that is, if you don't object," she added quickly.

He dragged his eyes from a remote spot in the valley and looked at her. "Thanks, but you didn't come here for that. I hired you to cook, nothing more."

His voice held an edge, and Robin knew she had just overstepped the boundary between them, even though she was trying her best to be gentle.

She was tempted to let it go at that, but something inside her pressed harder. It was her basic nature to help children, and here were two little boys desperately in need of a female figure, and the father didn't seem too far behind. He said the teachers had been patient and understanding with Zack; she was a teacher. Perhaps she could afford to stretch her patience a bit as well.

"You don't understand. I adore children, and I have a calling to work with them. When I'm not preparing meals, I'd much rather play with them or teach them something than sit around with my hands folded. All my life I was accused of being a tomboy." Her eyes twinkled. "And somewhere along the way the word hyper was added. I'm happiest when I'm busy."

She smiled at him, but he only half smiled in return. Why was he so hesitant to accept her help? He almost seemed to resent her offer, rather than be thankful for it.

"Well, I guess I could scrub up all the pots and pans, maybe tear out the old shelf lining and put in new. Or the floors? Want me to get down and wax the floors? And the stove, I could clean the oven again..."

This time the full lips softened, widened, and to her utter amazement, he began to chuckle. It warmed her heart to see the man laugh. She had almost wondered if he had made a vow never to smile or laugh after losing his wife.

"You know something?" She got up and walked over to his side, gently touching his arm. She couldn't seem to stop herself from reaching out to him; she was pulled like a magnet to offer comfort and support. At least that's what she thought she was offering.

"What?" he said, as his eyes dropped to her hand.

"Laughter is good for the soul. You should try it more often." He was leaning forward, his boot propped on the porch railing, his arm draped over his leg. Slowly, his hand came around, touching her fingers, lifting the arm she had burned.

"Does it feel better?" His voice was soft and soothing, like a gentle rain, and the tenderness in his eyes reached deep into her soul.

"Yes, it's fine."

His eyes returned to her face, trailing over every feature, settling finally on her lips. He moved forward half an inch, or did she merely imagine it? And he was still staring at her lips in a way that made her think he would kiss her any minute.

Kiss her any minute? She gently removed her hand, glancing toward the yard. She could see Will tagging Zack, and now Zack was running toward the porch. What on earth would they think if they should look up and see her holding hands with their dad? Or kissing him back—and she feared she would if he made the move.

"Well, guess I'd better go in," she said. This time it was she who was taking the formal approach, and he stared after her, his eyes darkening. "Leftovers okay for supper?" she called back.

"Leftovers will be fine. And Robin?"

She hesitated at the door, holding her breath, wondering what he was about to say.

"Thanks for singing hymns to the boys this morning—to all of us, in fact. Everyone enjoyed your music."

She smiled, touched by the compliment. "I'm glad. Maybe next Sunday I'll do it again if you don't object."

"On the contrary. I'll look forward to it."

Twelve

❧

R obin was just finishing in the kitchen when Zack poked his head around the door.

"We got a Monopoly set," he announced, his eyes probing hers.

"Oh, you do?" She glanced into the dining room where Will stood by the buffet watching her. That look of quiet longing pulled at her, and she hesitated, scratching her head.

"Do you have plenty of hotels?" she asked, pretending to look worried. "I like to put hotels on my property."

From the corner of her eye, she saw Will opening the drawer, removing the Monopoly set.

"I can beat you," Zack challenged, just in case she changed her mind.

She smiled down at him. He was a very bright little boy; he had already figured out some things about her nature.

"We have lotsa hotels," Will said, carefully counting them.

Will was bright too, in a quiet introspective way, just like his father.

"Then I guess we'd better get to it," she quipped, thinking that the letter to her mom at Seascape could wait.

Will efficiently removed the game and all its contents from the box while Robin and Zack settled down at the dining room table. Robin let her glance stray toward the closed door down the hall. Again, Craig had retreated to his office to do some work. Was it possible that he hibernated in there to avoid her?

Don't be so conceited, she told herself, dismissing the thought as silly. Still, if by chance he was trying to avoid her, fine. In fact, she would be relieved to know that. At times she felt that her presence was more an inconvenience than a help. There was tension beneath the surface when they were together, which made them both uncomfortable. Was it because he had hired her out of politeness? Had she accepted in order to stay on this ranch with its sentimental value? At first that was the case, she was certain of it. But now there seemed to be an underlying reason for staying, and she wasn't sure why.

"Well, it's your turn." Zack was breathless with excitement. Robin could see he loved the game.

She had been staring at the paper money in her hand, her thoughts on the man down the hall, rather than the game.

"I'm planning my strategy," she countered, "so you guys better be on your toes."

The game lasted for two hours and ended about the time Will began to yawn and Zack turned grouchy over his losses.

Passing through to the kitchen to refill his coffee cup, Craig assessed the situation and announced bedtime.

"You guys have had a long day," he said in a gentle voice.

"And tomorrow we're going to the Waltons," practical Will pointed out. For a moment, Robin looked blankly at Craig, who seemed at a loss for a second or two, then he nodded his head.

"You're right. So off to bed."

For once, Zack didn't offer a protest as he and Will put away the game and pushed the chairs back in place.

"Well, good night, guys," Robin said as they trudged off.

Her eyes slipped farther down the hall to the office door, closed again. She tried to forget about Craig as she went to her room, thinking now she would write that letter. Instead, she felt an ache in her shoulders and decided that what she needed was a hot bath. Since the generator was still on, she decided to take advantage of it. She gathered up her nightclothes and toiletries, then slipped across to the bathroom.

As she ran the hot water and stepped into the clawfoot tub, she thought about the boys and the Monopoly game. Settling into the hot water and feeling her shoulders relax, she let her thoughts stray back to Craig. He had his own bathroom back there somewhere, so she didn't have to smell his aftershave or cologne. Just a whiff of that delightfully spicy stuff was enough to tantalize her. She didn't want to get any closer to the man's possessions. Or to the man. No, she definitely didn't want to do that...

What should I do? Craig wondered as he lay in the darkness of his bedroom, his hands folded behind his head on the pillow. Deep in his heart, he kept hoping there was a way he and the boys could hang on to the ranch. After poring over his ledgers all weekend, he had come to terms with the cold, hard facts: There was no way he could survive another winter without getting a loan. His parents did well to live on their small pension after retiring, and he was too proud to ask his father-in-law for money, although he had plenty to spare. What Frank Tidwell wanted was his grandsons back in Seattle.

Craig's head ached with the burden of worry. In his heart he knew that returning to Seattle was not the answer to his problems, but he had to think of his sons.

His mind circled back to the possibility of a loan. He had spoken with Mr. Spencer at the bank in Cranbrook last week. While the man had not been encouraging about an operating loan, he had given Craig a handful of papers to fill out and invited him to return for another conversation.

A glance through those papers had been enough to discourage him. A financial statement would reveal his dwindling funds while giving proof that he had a lot to learn about cattle farming. Once he returned from the bank, he had shoved the papers in his desk drawer and started thinking of Seattle once again. And then Robin Grayson had appeared and thrown him off balance for a day or two.

Robin Grayson. One more little problem to add to the heap. She was beginning to get under his skin. After today, there was no denying that she was a very good person, someone he was glad for the boys to know. And he was glad to know her as well.

Still, he had chosen to avoid her this evening because he knew he was beginning to have feelings for her. The kind of warm fuzzy feelings that could get a man in trouble fast. He had known two hours after she arrived at Sundance that he liked her, genuinely liked her. Since yesterday afternoon, however, he was beginning to fear that something more than *like* was creeping into his heart.

When he entered the house, he found himself looking for her, and when she greeted him with that cute little smile and a sparkle in those hazel eyes...Well, it made him miss Brenda more than ever. Or not so much anymore. Which was it?

He rolled over on his side, trying to shut out all the worries that hammered at him day and night. Maybe tomorrow would be a better day...

Thirteen

On Monday morning Craig picked up the phone and called the bank in Cranbrook to schedule an appointment with the bank manager for Tuesday. That would give him one day to fill out a financial statement, organize his thoughts, iron a dress shirt, and prepare himself to ask for an operating loan. Beg, if necessary.

In spite of his worries, he had slept soundly for the first time in weeks. A fun-filled Sunday with the boys and Robin had helped him. He was glad to see Sam happy and to watch Lucille and her daughter have a good time. That was what he had wanted to do with a ranch: entertain friends, ride horses, lounge on the front porch, and rest his eyes on his land. He had almost given up on that dream until this morning.

When he woke up and looked at the sunrise, a strange new hope had taken root in his heart. He felt a surge of strength flow back into his beaten soul, and now he was ready to pull himself up from the ground and give life another ride.

Whether he would admit it or not, he suspected Robin Grayson had something to do with this new feeling. He had actually been whistling in the barn that morning when he bumped into Sam, who gawked at him as though he had met up with a stranger. Then a silly little grin tilted Sam's mouth. To Craig's great relief, Sam kept his thoughts, or his suspicions, to himself.

Now the smell of coffee brewing told Craig she was up. He'd already gone through one pot, beginning with his first cup at 6:00 A.M. Standing, he circled the desk and opened the door. As he passed the boys' bedrooms, he saw them sleeping peacefully. He should wake them, since it was after eight, but he was relishing the thought of a quiet cup of coffee with Robin.

She was puttering around the kitchen, dressed in a Disney World T-shirt and a pair of Levi's. When he walked through the door, she turned with a look of surprise.

"Hi. I thought you had already gone to the barn," she said.

"Been there, done that," he grinned, pulling back a kitchen chair and taking a seat. "So Kathy at the bank is your cousin?" he asked suddenly.

"Third, I think, depending on how you count." She laughed as she poured him a cup of coffee. "You see, Skook and his brother rode into this country together. They decided they didn't want to be wheat farmers like the rest of the family," she said, taking a seat at the table. "They took off down to the States, worked their way back into British Columbia, and just kept on riding until they found this wonderful place. Skook sent back for Jenny, and Uncle Chuck got married to Irene, who was from Fort Steele. She didn't like the ranch, so he sold his half to Skook."

Craig nodded, listening attentively.

"Kathy's father, Doug Spencer, was Chuck Russell's grandson. Let's see, his mother and my grandmother were cousins. He's a few years younger than Mom, and I met him for the first time this week. I don't really know him. He was in a meeting when I stopped in at the bank, but he did come out to say hello." She sipped her coffee and shrugged. "He seemed a bit formal, and I couldn't bring myself to address him as 'uncle.' But I adore Kathy."

Craig was thinking about the word *formal,* not liking the implications. Mr. Spencer had impressed him exactly the same way, and he found himself dreading another encounter with him tomorrow—but he had no choice.

"Kathy seems pleasant," he said, switching subjects. "Like you, she has a sense of humor. Had you met her before you two framed me?"

Robin laughed, taking no offense. He seemed to be in a jovial mood, and it relaxed her. "No, I wrote to her, asking her to help me find a summer job. I explained the only reason I was coming was to kick around this ranch. She called and invited me to come for a visit. And then, when I arrived, she surprised me with the good news that you'd been into the bank and mentioned to her your cook had broken his leg."

He nodded. "I really hadn't thought about a replacement until the day I went to the bank. I was burning the candle at both ends, chasing after the boys, grocery shopping and cooking, and trying to carry on the usual ranch chores. She made you sound like the answer to my prayers."

Maybe I am, she wanted to reply. "Obviously, that can be debated," she answered, "but where Kathy is concerned, we've become great friends already. It seems like I've known her for years, and we do have a daring sense of humor," she said, smiling across at him. "She didn't lie about my age, did she? I mean —what exactly did she say?"

"Come to think of it, it's what she didn't say!"

"Oh well, there doesn't seem to be any harm done. You're

putting up with my cooking, and I'm having a great time."

He chuckled at that as his eyes strayed over the kitchen. "I haven't seen the kitchen this clean since the realtor showed it to me!"

"How long ago was that?" Robin asked.

"About a year and a half." He looked back at her. "Your cooking is fine, and you get along well with the boys. I appreciate your efforts."

"It's fun for me. Are you hungry?"

Noting his hesitation, Robin opened the refrigerator door and pulled out a huge bowl. "Pancake batter," she said. "Most boys like pancakes."

"And men."

Robin hesitated. The cold bowl pressed into her palm while a warmth crept up her cheeks. She looked into his face and saw that nice smile again. Robin hated to keep referring to the fact that a smile sat well on his face, so she said nothing. She merely made a mental note to do what she could to keep that smile coming. It really made a difference.

Suddenly the thing that had been bothering her came back to mind. "May I ask you something personal? You can tell me it's none of my business, and I won't be offended."

He leaned back in the chair, his head tilted to one side. "Shoot."

"It's about your wife," she swallowed. Automatically, her eyes drifted to the picture in the living room. "I was curious about what happened to her. It would help me understand the boys better," she quickly added, not to mention their father.

He sighed. "She suffered an aneurysm to her brain. She was in a coma for eleven weeks." He shook his head slowly and stared into space. "She neglected checkups. She rushed one of us to the doctor the first time we coughed, but she never took time to go herself. I should have insisted. But she was always boasting about how great she felt."

Robin saw the agony in his face. She bit her lip, uncertain what to say.

She knew those words must be painful for him. "I am so sorry, Craig," Robin said, leaning across the table to wrap her fingers around his broad hand. In sharing his despair it did not occur to her that she had done two things for the first time: she had called him Craig, and she had held his hand.

"Thanks," he said in a low voice, staring into his coffee cup. "Brenda and I had talked about buying some land in Canada; it was a dream she shared with me. After she died, I couldn't bear to go on living in the same house in Omak. We had a small ranch there, but I put it on the market, got a quick offer, and packed up the boys and left."

He lifted his eyes and stared out the window. "In retrospect it was a hasty thing to do, but at the time I just couldn't bear the grief and the memories. And I thought a change would be good for the boys and me."

"I think you did the right thing coming here," she said kindly, desperately wanting to speak the right words. She had never in her life felt so sorry for anyone, nor had she seen such grief and despair in a person's face. It wrenched her heart, and she squeezed his hand a bit tighter. "This is a beautiful ranch, and it's nice to think of the boys growing up here."

Upon hearing those words, Craig closed his eyes and shook his head.

"What is it?" she asked, withdrawing her hand, for she could see she had struck a nerve.

"I'm not sure they'll be growing up here."

"Why not?" She was amazed to hear his words. Zack and Will—and Craig, of course—seemed to love the ranch.

He hesitated, draining his cup. "Their grandparents in Seattle want them back down there in a big way. My folks are older and have plenty of grandkids, but Brenda only had one sister—and she doesn't want children."

"I see." Robin sat quietly for a moment, considering what he had told her. "So Zack and Will are their only grandchildren, and this is pretty far to come for a visit. Do the boys visit them?" she asked, then suddenly remembered Zack's angry outburst about his grandmother.

"Not enough. Frank and Betsy, the grandparents, drove up to see us last year. They arrived, unannounced, on a terrible winter day. There was snow and ice all over the place, and the wind chill was about twenty below. Naturally, the boys were home from school, sick with colds. That was enough to convince Betsy that we had no business living up here..."

Footsteps bounded down the hall, and Zack rushed into the kitchen, his hair sprouting in all directions. "I'm hungry!"

"Then what about pancakes?" Robin asked.

"Wow! I'll get Will up."

"Better let me," Craig came to his feet. "Will can be a bit cranky first thing, particularly when you jump on top of him!"

Robin was pleased that the somber conversation had not left him depressed. She turned back to the stove, trying to force her mind toward pancakes and bacon, but she kept thinking about everything he had told her. And she was beginning to understand why the worried frown had almost become a permanent fixture.

Breakfast was lively, with the conversation centering around the day's events.

"I can't wait to play video games," Zack said around a mouthful of pancake.

"Zack, you be good," his father cautioned. "And you watch

him, Will. You both know if you don't behave yourselves you may not get a second invitation."

"You're coming too, aren't you?" Will looked at his dad.

"Actually, I have work to do. I'll drive you guys over, and I'll ask when I should come back. I don't want you wearing out your welcome at the Walton house."

"But aren't you gonna have some of that cake?" Zack stared in disbelief.

Craig grinned. "Maybe when I come after you. Now finish your pancakes before they get cold."

After they had said their good-byes and driven off, Robin decided to mop the floor, a task she didn't relish, but dirt tracks necessitated it. Through the screen door in the kitchen, she could hear Sam hammering away on one of the outbuildings. She had heard Craig mention putting up a new roof and replacing a door on the bunkhouse.

As she went about her work, she tried to imagine what life was like here in the winter with just Craig and the boys, and Sam and Harley at the bunkhouse. They definitely needed a woman.

As the floor dried, she wandered into the living room and stared at the gold-framed picture of the woman who had married Craig and given birth to two fine boys.

She was a beauty, Robin decided, aware she could not compete in that department. There was a fragile look to her heart-shaped face and small features. The white-blond hair and blue eyes had been replicated on Zack's face, and she imagined it must be painful for Craig, at times, just to look into the little boy's face and see his late wife looking back.

Sighing, she turned away and went to the bathroom to freshen up. As she heard the roar of Craig's truck returning, she gathered up her courage and met him out in the driveway.

"Since the boys are gone this afternoon, I was wondering if it would be okay for me to hike back to the cabin Skook built."

Craig's eyes ran down her slim body, then turned toward the upper end of the valley. "Sure. Tell you what, I'll saddle up Sugar for you. He's a gentle Appaloosa." He looked back at her. "You do like horses?"

"I'm crazy about horses, but are you sure it's okay? I mean—"

"Of course it's okay. The last mile of that road would be impassable in your car. As for hiking, it's over three miles and pretty steep in places. You'll enjoy riding Sugar," he said.

She needed no further persuasion. "Okay, if you don't mind," she said, glancing toward her room. "I'll change clothes."

Later, as Robin hurried toward the barn, she spotted two horses saddled and waiting. Craig stepped into view, giving the horses some feed. She stopped walking. Someone was going with her. She doubted it was Sam.

Smiling to herself, she turned and hurried back to the kitchen. She quickly made up some sandwiches, grabbed a couple of apples, and added two cans of soda to the paper sack. As an afterthought, she popped in a roll of paper towels.

Then she set off toward the barn, humming a popular love song and thinking about how romantic it would be to see the Russell cabin with a man like Craig beside her.

The thought was a bit dizzying, and her steps slowed as another set of warning signals went off in her head.

Be careful, Robin. This guy could be gone with your heart before you knew it was missing.

Fourteen

৵৶

H i," she called as Craig straightened the reins on the big sorrel.

"Hi." For a moment, he felt embarrassed as her eyes moved toward both horses, saddled and waiting.

"That's a fine-looking animal," she said, indicating the sorrel.

"Name's Chief. He's my horse."

Robin nodded, stroking the white blaze on the horse's forehead.

"The other one is Sugar. He's yours for the afternoon."

"I like him." She glanced from Sugar to Chief. "I brought along a snack, and apples for the horses."

"I decided I'd better go with you." He frowned. "There are grizzlies in this country." His eyes fell to the sack in her hands. "And if you're taking along food, you might be inviting trouble."

He was uncomfortably aware that she might see right through him to his simple desire to spend some time with her. But if she did, she wasn't letting on. "Well, I'm glad you can come with me. I hope I'm not interrupting your plans."

He felt a little grin tugging at the corner of his mouth. "I need to be interrupted. I've been doing the kind of paperwork I despise." He adjusted his dark Stetson on his head and looked up at the sky. "It's a pretty day, and a ride will clear my head."

As Craig spoke those words, he glanced at Robin and wondered if this little outing would clear his head or mess it up. He was taking a risk just being with her, but he had decided to think of her as someone nice but temporary passing through his life. After hearing her sing those hymns with such conviction, he felt good about having Robin spend time with the boys, and he was well aware that some of that goodness might touch him. He needed it.

"Here, let me take that." He reached for the sack, then looked surprised at its weight. "Feels like you won't go hungry."

"I have a big appetite," she smiled, turning to Sugar. She had strapped her camera around her neck and had just loaded it with film. "You're my first subject," she said to Chief, as she snapped his picture. "And you're next," she said, turning to Craig.

"Chief is more photogenic than I am," Craig replied, placing the sack lunch in his saddlebag. "Give you a leg up?" he asked, glancing over his shoulder.

"Nope, I'm already there." The tan saddle creaked beneath her weight as she leaned forward to stroke the Appaloosa's silky mane. "Hi, Sugar."

Glancing back, she noticed how easily he swung into the saddle, as though he had been born there.

"We're off," he said, turning Chief's head toward the trail across the meadow. "The cabin's about three miles from here. The road runs beside the creek and climbs to what we call Middle Meadow, where the valley opens wide, then we'll cross the creek and climb again. Anytime you want to stop and rest, just let me know."

"I think I'm as excited about this as Zack is over video games," Robin said, tilting her head back to look up at a pure blue sky. "I hope the boys have a good time."

Craig smiled. "I must have warned them a dozen times to behave themselves. I'm sure Mrs. Walton was expecting the worst the minute I was out of sight."

"Then she'll be pleasantly surprised. And what about the daughter who made the chocolate cake?" she teased.

"I didn't meet her."

"Too bad."

"Mr. Walton insisted I let the boys stay until this evening," he continued smoothly.

"At which time you'll get some cake." Robin couldn't resist teasing him, although she wasn't sure how he would take it.

"Do I detect some sarcasm there?" He grinned at her.

Robin liked the way the skin crinkled at the edges of his eyes when he was amused. He was so different when he relaxed and tried to enjoy himself. It made her want to be as witty as possible, just to keep a smile on his face.

Looking at her profile, Craig felt something move slowly across his heart. Like a chunk of ice beginning to melt. Beneath her red-gold hair, her features were delicate and well-shaped. There was just a sprinkle of freckles across the bridge of her nose which added to her wholesome look. She wore nice boots, Levi's, and a white shirt.

"Do you burn easily?" His eyes lingered on her pale skin.

"I came prepared," she said, reaching into the back pocket of her jeans and withdrawing a baseball cap.

"You're a Braves fan?" he asked.

"Why not? When I was living in Charleston, some friends

got tickets to a game, and we went to Atlanta. It was great. After that, I watched all their games on TV." She tugged the cap lower on her forehead.

He thought she looked even cuter with the cap. It seemed to go with her personality and spirit; he wondered if he could continue to think of her as a "temporary" person in their lives. That brought another worried frown.

"Well," she said, looking back at him, "at last I'm doing what I've wanted to do for years. I'm on a horse, riding back to see the place Skook homesteaded."

A breeze moved over the meadow, bringing the sweet smell of meadow grass and a cooling moisture from the creek. Craig took a deep breath and realized he felt better than he had in a long time. In fact, he felt wonderful.

"Some of my friends have told me I'm melodramatic about my ancestors," she said, "but it's always been important to me to trace my roots." Her eyes skimmed the distant mountains. "Maybe it was my grandmother's knack for telling stories that fired my imagination or the fact that I love horses and could easily imagine myself galloping though the wilds of British Columbia."

She laughed easily as she spoke, and Craig felt the tension slipping away. She was an easy person to like, to relate to, unlike many women with whom he had little in common.

"Did you do a lot of riding growing up?" he asked conversationally.

"Yes and no. We lived in town, and Dad kept reminding me that town was no place for a horse when I begged for one every summer." She shrugged lightly, grinning at Craig. "He paid for riding lessons and stable fees for me; my two sisters wanted party dresses and shoes."

She leaned forward in the saddle, sitting the horse well, Craig thought. "Do your parents still live in Calgary?"

Robin frowned, studying the reins in her hands. "No, Dad died a couple of years ago, and Mom was devastated. She now spends her winters in Florida, helping a friend run a bed and breakfast. Seascape is the name of the B&B. Doesn't that sound nice?"

"Sure does. I'm sorry about your dad. How did he die?"

She swallowed. "We thought he was in perfect health. Then he had a massive heart attack while mowing the lawn. I guess that's the easy way," she said, looking at Craig with pain-filled eyes. "Anyway, I wish I hadn't complained so much about wanting a horse."

Craig looked into her eyes and glimpsed a little girl kind of hurt still lurking there. He reached over to touch her shoulder. Most of the time she seemed so independent. This was the first time he had felt a need to console her, since that first night when she burned her arm. "I think your father was right about town being no place for a horse. I personally think it's cruel to pen up an animal meant to run free."

She looked thoughtful as he spoke, then slowly she began to nod. "I agree. That's why I appreciate this opportunity so much. Thanks, Craig."

"You're welcome." They were approaching the creek, and that was a blessing, Craig decided. He needed to be diverted from the feelings rolling over him, feelings for Robin Grayson, feelings he must not feel.

"We have to cross the creek again," he inclined his head, speaking rather gruffly, "and the trail starts to get steep, so hang on to your cap."

The horses splashed through the creek and climbed a slight incline leading to another high grass valley.

"Sundance," Craig said as they rode through the valley. "It's a good name. I think of it when I see the way the sun dances over the rocks and across the meadow."

"But that isn't why the ranch was named Sundance."

He shifted in his saddle, looking at her curiously. "Oh no? You got some inside information you'd like to share?"

"Well, as I told you before, Skook and his brother Chuck had decided they didn't want to be wheat farmers, so they saddled up and road out of South Saskatchewan down through Montana looking for work. In the northeast corner of Wyoming, they found a ranch they liked near the town of Sundance; but things didn't work out for them."

She shrugged, glancing at Craig. "I don't know what happened, but they left there and worked their way across Wyoming and up through Idaho into British Columbia. When Skook found this property, he knew this was what he had searched for all of his life. He wrote to my great-grandmother to tell her he was coming back to get her. 'I've found my Sundance,' he said."

Craig nodded thoughtfully, staring ahead as the cabin came into view. "I know exactly how he felt."

"Craig, why do you think Skook chose this particular spot in British Columbia?"

Craig leaned back in the saddle and looked around. "Probably for the same reason I did. You see how the creek centers the meadows on each side, making it easy to irrigate? And those steep mountains rise on both sides of the valley floor, providing a natural fence line for cattle. So you have water, with little irrigation to be done, meadowland, and natural boundaries. It's a perfect spot for a ranch."

They had climbed to the middle meadow, then ridden through woods into a higher meadow.

"This is known as Skook's meadow," Craig grinned at her.

"And there's one last meadow up there, a high one that's known as Horsethief Park."

Robin had been snapping pictures all along, but now she looked straight ahead and her breath caught.

Beyond a log fence, in a grove of cottonwoods, sat the cabin. She lifted her camera and began to snap more pictures.

They slowed the horses at the pole fence surrounding the cabin and drew rein.

Robin swung down and walked over and touched the old wooden fence curiously.

Craig said, "The fence was probably built to keep the cattle from getting to the cabin, stepping on the porch, or trying to claim it as their barn."

The fence had been repaired and reworked, judging from the aged logs; some had decayed several years before, but using smaller poles, the fence had been braced.

Robin was snapping more pictures. "I can't wait to get these developed and start my scrapbook." She turned to the cabin. "Isn't it incredible?" she glanced at Craig. "Built so long ago and yet it's still standing."

"And it's actually in pretty good shape."

They walked toward the log cabin, built out of eight-to-ten-inch logs, thick and well placed, notched on the corners. The logs were tightly fitted and weatherproofed with a combination of mud and grass caulking.

"As you can see," Craig pointed, "the roof has been repaired with half a dozen different colors over the years."

Robin tilted her head back and looked at the patchwork roof, which had an overall appearance of red tarpaper.

"And that tin stovepipe in the back corner was probably added to accommodate an old sheepherder's stove, used for heat as well as cooking."

Robin snapped another picture. "You think the roof leaks?"

"Nope. I was here one of those rare days when it rains. All that patching up there has worked," Craig said as their boots sank into the thick carpet of grass leading to the front of the cabin. "And it's the secret to the way the walls have been preserved."

"Do you come up here very much, Craig?" Was it possible that someone else could be as taken with this place as she was? From the serene expression that had slipped over Craig's features, she guessed that he was every bit as fascinated as she.

"I've only been a few times," he answered, "but it always recharges my batteries to ride up here and think and dream."

They paused at the eight-foot porch, whose roof sat up higher than the rest of the cabin and was covered with large shingles. "I think this was added by the second, or maybe third owner. It changes the looks of the cabin somewhat, but it provides a place to sit and get out of the weather," Craig said as Robin stepped onto the porch.

"I like it. Especially the porch furniture!"

The "furniture" consisted of three logs sawed into twenty-inch pieces, turned onto their ends, and used as stools.

"And it's personalized," she laughed, pointing to the initials carved on the side of one of the logs. She looked curiously at the metal framework of bars crisscrossing the two windows, evenly spaced on each side of the door.

"That's to keep grizzlies out," he said.

Robin shivered involuntarily, glancing back over her shoulder. "There are some still around?"

"Oh yeah, but not like there were years ago. They used to tear windows out of cabins to get inside; then they'd tear up the cabin, looking for food."

"Could we change the subject?" She approached the front

door. It was shorter than a normal door, although about the same width.

"Did you see that?" Craig pointed.

Over the door, carved into the log in three-inch letters, were the words SKOOK 1908.

"Do you think that's when he completed the cabin?" Robin glanced at Craig.

"Probably."

Robin stood on tiptoe, tracing each notched letter with her forefinger.

Pushing the door open, Craig ducked under and entered. He held the door wide, letting in abundant light, and he motioned Robin in. She entered and looked around, her eyes moving slowly over every inch of the cabin.

A bed constructed of poles leaned against the left wall, with its mattress half on, half off. In the back corner she could see an old wood-burning stove, and on the opposite side of the room, a table missing one leg was propped against the wall. A chair with a broken back sat by the table.

Strewn across the floor were leaves and pine cones and bits of cotton from the mattress. A few old pans still hung on wooden stakes in the cracks between the logs that formed the walls.

"It's actually in pretty good shape," Craig said, walking over to anchor the table against the wall. "In fact, I would say it's probably livable if it was cleaned up and the furniture was replaced."

Robin was filled with emotion as she looked around the room, trying to imagine her great-grandparents there. Her eyes returned to the bed, wondering if that was the bed her beloved grandmother had slept in.

"My grandmother was born in this room," she said, looking back at Craig. "I loved her dearly; she was wonderful to me.

She died several years ago, but standing here now, I can still hear her voice, small yet clear, telling me about her early years at Sundance."

The afternoon sunshine slanted through the door, touching the right side of her face. She turned her back to Craig, so he wouldn't see the glint of tears in her eyes, and stared at the bed.

Taking a deep breath, she reached down and picked up a small pine cone and dropped it in her pocket. Then she sauntered back to the door. As they walked onto the porch again, she tilted her head back to look up at the name and date.

"I remember a couple of old pictures Granny had of her father," she said. "Skook was a giant of a man, six foot four, two hundred and fifty pounds, with black wavy hair and a full beard."

"He's quite a legend among the old-timers," Craig said. "He and his brother Chuck."

Craig walked across the rough-planked porch and stepped onto the lush grass that led to the creek bank. "I've often wondered what this country was like before the first white man ever rode into the valley." He walked over to a big cottonwood and sat down, picking up bits of gravel and flipping them into the eddied pool.

Robin followed, taking a seat beside him. "I know. Me, too." She drew her knees up to her chest, wrapping her arms around them. "Craig, this was the right spot for the cabin, wasn't it?"

He nodded, looking around. "It's placed on a knoll out of heavy runoff in the spring when the snows melt, and it's away from high water. That big cut bank over there breaks the wind, and the grove of cottonwoods shades the cabin in summer. Still, there's plenty of sun."

He touched her shoulder. "If you lean over this way and look down the valley, you can see for miles, from mountaintop to mountaintop." She had her camera up, snapping one picture after another. Removing the strap from around her head, she turned to place the camera on a smooth rock nearby, but in the process, the camera slipped from her hand.

"Oops." Craig grabbed the camera just as her hand closed over it. They were both gripping the camera, with their faces inches apart.

Turning the camera loose, Craig looked at her soft lips and wondered how it would be to kiss her. He decided to find out. He dipped his head and kissed her gently. Then he put an arm around her shoulder, steadying her, and he kissed her again.

Fifteen

❧

Startled by the sudden rush of emotions she felt, Robin finally pulled back and looked into Craig's eyes, seeing a strange mix of emotion there.

She could be playing with fire and she knew it, and she looked away, trying to collect her thoughts.

"Sorry if I was out of line," he said.

He stood up, walked away from her, and stared at the cabin.

"Craig, I'm glad you came with me today," she said, standing up, slinging her camera around her shoulder.

Robin wanted him to know she liked being with him, but she didn't want to get into something that was wrong for both of them. And she still wasn't sure how she felt about him.

He glanced back over his shoulder. "You sure about that?"

"Yep," she smiled, "I'm sure." She took a deep breath and looked at the weatherbeaten cabin. "Granny told me that Skook's wife, Jenny, had lots of hardships here. They lost a baby son..."

Craig nodded, looking around the peaceful setting. "I'm sure it was a rough life at times. The snow would have been deep, the winters hard..."

"Yet Jenny was always so strong. I'm sure it was because she drew deeply on her faith. Granny gave me Jenny's Bible with her favorite verses inscribed inside the cover; one verse, in particular, was a favorite."

Craig walked back to her and looked into her eyes. "What was it?"

"For the LORD God is a sun and a shield: the LORD will give grace and glory: no good thing will he withhold from them that walk uprightly." Robin turned her eyes from the cabin up to Craig. "Come to think of it, that verse has sustained my family from one generation to another."

Craig repeated the verse and felt emotion squeezing his heart. "You know," he said quietly, "I need to be saying that verse and a few others. I'm a Christian, or I claimed to be when I was growing up. Then after Brenda and I married, I always found an excuse to skip church on Sundays. I was trying to get a small ranch up and going, but that was just an excuse."

Brenda! And here he was kissing Robin Grayson, thinking about a relationship with her. He didn't want a relationship with Robin, or with any woman, for that matter. There was too much risk involved; the chance of a broken heart was not worth the price he would have to pay.

His eyes drifted back to the cabin as he recalled the kind of woman Brenda had been, the legacy she had left for them in her faith. He regretted not sharing Brenda's faith; in fact, it made him sick at heart. He certainly wanted that kind of faith for his sons, and he knew he must set the example.

"You're blessed to be living up here," Robin said.

"Excuse me?" Craig blinked, pulling his thoughts back to the moment and feeling slightly embarrassed that he wasn't paying attention.

"I said you're blessed to live here."

As her words registered, a look of sadness slipped over his face. "I know, but I'm not sure I'm going to stay." He surprised himself by admitting that; Robin was visibly even more surprised.

"Not stay? But...why? I mean, I thought you and the boys loved it here."

He was pacing nervously, kicking at a rock. "As I mentioned before, all ranchers have weather problems. An early snow came before I got the hay up, and I went into winter short of feed. By spring I had to sell my cattle."

He stopped talking and chewed the inside of his lower lip. Why had he told her personal things about his finances? He felt the pressure of her hand on his arm.

"That sounds like quite a challenge," she said. "I can understand why you've seemed so worried at times."

"Yeah, and the Tillmans keep calling with a subtle reminder that Brenda wouldn't want the boys raised here."

Robin caught her breath. That might be the toughest part for him. "I suppose they would like to see you move back to the States," she said gently.

His mouth twisted bitterly. "You got it." He took a deep breath and stared up at the sky, so pure and blue that it seemed like a painting.

"Craig, it's your call, you know. You're their father, and I think you are managing quite well. The boys seem happy."

"We could be doing better," he said quietly.

"Everyone could be doing better. We just do the best we can wherever we choose to live." Then she thought of something else. "Where would you go if you left here?"

"Seattle, maybe."

Robin arched a brow. "Craig, you don't mean that. You

122

wouldn't really give up this ranch and go back to Seattle?"

He hated to give up and go back to Seattle, and he hated to admit he couldn't make it on his own. He looked away, uncomfortable about how far this conversation had strayed. It was not his nature to get so personal with someone, particularly someone he did not know well—like Robin Grayson.

Now she straightened up, drew a deep breath, and looked around for a moment, almost as if she sensed that she had overstepped her boundaries and it was time to change the subject.

"Hey, I'm starving," she said. "What about you?"

"I suppose."

She plunged into the lunch sack and withdrew two wrapped sandwiches.

Craig grinned. "Were you planning to eat all that by yourself?"

"Two sandwiches? That's no big deal."

"And two cans of soda?"

"Okay, so I saw you saddling both horses and took a chance that you were coming," she laughed. "Was I being too presumptuous?"

He chuckled. "I don't think so. I'd hate to sit and watch you eat."

The serious mood was finally broken, and they munched on their sandwiches.

"You know," Robin said, looking around her, "I can easily imagine Skook and Jenny Russell here and my grandmother playing in the yard."

"You really are fascinated with this place, aren't you?"

"Yes, I am." She sighed, closing her eyes and breathing deeply of the fresh, pine-scented air. "I could stay here forever."

He stared at her as he took a sip of his soda. It was strange how she kept getting prettier and prettier to him. Or perhaps it was knowing the kind of person she seemed to be that made her even more attractive.

She had been asking him some personal questions; he decided that gave him the right to ask her a few in return.

"Will you be returning to Charleston to teach?"

"No," she shook her head. "I enjoyed living in the States, but Canada is home to me."

"So you're going back to Calgary?"

She rolled the canned soda between her palms. "Yes, I'll probably teach there next year. I've applied to the board of education, but there isn't an opening yet. There's a chance one lady may be moving to Vancouver, but it's nothing definite. I can always fill in as a substitute for a while. I'm hoping for a small place."

He nodded, thinking it over. Somehow it bothered him to know that she would be staying in Canada. It was easier to write her off if he thought she would be thousands of miles away in the fall.

Craig reflected on how fortunate he was to have met Robin. When he kissed her, he had been surprised by his feelings for her. As much as he kept telling himself that love was not worth the pain, he kept feeling a new kind of joy taking root in his heart.

It felt good. Maybe he should stop being so frightened by a relationship; maybe he should gather up his courage and try to love again. Glancing at the woman beside him, he thought it might be very easy to love Robin Grayson.

She finished her drink and picked up their sandwich wrappers, placing them neatly in the sack.

"I'd like to go through the cabin one more time," she said.

"Sure. I'll get the horses ready."

Craig thought maybe she would like to have a little time

124

alone with her thoughts. She smiled and hesitated, as though she wanted to say something. Instead, she turned up the path to the cabin.

Robin walked away from him, thinking what a wonderful afternoon it had been. While this place was sentimental to her, she knew that Craig was part of the reason she was having such a good time. There was something growing between them; she could feel it. Or was it only her imagination?

By the time she joined him again, both were in a quiet, thoughtful mood. They rode back in a comfortable silence, each basking in the enchantment of the day they had shared, at ease with one another.

And as the house came into view, Robin wondered if she could somehow stay there forever.

♦

Sixteen

❧

It was early Tuesday afternoon, and the boys were playing a game of checkers while Robin looked over their school papers. She noticed how Zack's grades were mostly Cs with a D here and there; Will was a straight A student.

She frowned. Will's excellent grades did not help matters with Zack, she felt certain. Craig had left early for town, and she had volunteered to look after the boys while he was away.

"What are you guys interested in?" she asked, just as Zack crowned Will with red checkers. "Do you like science or math or—"

"Horses!" Zack interrupted her.

"I like science," Will replied seriously.

Robin nodded, looking back at Zack. "I'm going to tell you guys a story, and I want you to listen carefully."

She began a story about spaceships and rockets which captured Will's attention but left Zack wiggling and staring out the window. She cut that story short and looked at Zack. "This time, Zack, I'm going to tell you a story that ends with saving a wild mustang. But you have to listen in order to learn about the mustang."

Immediately, she had his attention, and although she used the same theme as the story about spaceships and rockets, she used animals instead and had Zack's undivided attention.

As she finished the story, the sound of a truck out in the driveway diverted their attention, and the boys glanced toward the door. Robin was looking that way, too, as the sound of boots echoed over the porch and Craig entered the living room.

The boys called out to him, and Robin smiled, but Craig's smile, like his words, was limited as he headed back to his office.

"Can we go out to play now?" Zack looked at Robin.

"If it's okay with your dad."

"Dad!" Zack raced down the hall after him while Robin picked up a magazine and began to flip through the pages. What was wrong with Craig? she wondered, staring blankly at the pages. He had left with a smile, whistling to himself on the way to his truck. When he returned, the old frown was nestled deep between his brows, and his eyes were tired and troubled.

Maybe he was hungry. She glanced at the wall clock. It was only three o'clock. She'd make some coffee.

As she got up and went to the kitchen, she told herself she simply had to get back to her decaffeinated tea bags. She was hyper enough without the caffeine; soon she'd be leaping off the walls, along with Zack.

Spooning coffee into the coffeemaker, she thought of Zack again, and pulled two mugs down from the cabinet. She wanted to talk with Craig about what she suspected.

The boys were racing through the living room, headed outside. Robin caught a glimpse of a football as they tore out the door with a bang.

She heard Craig's steps along the hall, and she turned as he entered the kitchen.

"How about some coffee?" she asked, hoping to erase the frown from his face.

"Just what I need." He took a seat at the kitchen table and looked across at her. "So what have you guys been doing?"

"Reading stories." She poured him a cup of coffee and limited herself to half a cup with lots of milk. "Craig, I want to talk to you about Zack."

His head shot up. "Now what's he done?"

"Nothing," she laughed. "He behaved himself quite well. No, what I wanted to say was...well, as I was reading to him I noticed his inability to follow the story when—"

"That's Zack," he said impatiently. "This past year, I was getting a note from the teacher every other day about how he wouldn't pay attention."

"I think there's a reason for it," she said.

Craig lifted a dark brow. "Changing schools?"

She shook her head. "No, I imagine Zack has always had a tendency for his mind to jump from one thing to another. I think he has attention deficit disorder."

"What?"

"Don't worry. It isn't anything that can't be handled."

"Attention deficit..." His voice trailed as his eyes lifted over her head to a remote spot behind her. "The kindergarten teacher in Omak mentioned that. She suggested a drug for him." He looked at Robin, and his eyes turned cold. "Look, I appreciate what you're doing here, but I'm not ready to start popping pills in Zack just because he's an active little boy."

"I didn't suggest that!" she said, taken aback by his gruff tone. "As a matter of fact, even if he had ADD, I wouldn't recommend—"

"And just what would you recommend, Miss Grayson? You seem to have all the answers, from Sunday school services to warm milk."

She came to her feet, glaring across the table at him. "I

resent that. And I don't have the answers for any of your problems. But the biggest problem I see is your attitude! And only you can change that."

She whipped around the table and sped down the hall to her room, closing the door. She pounced on the bed, drawing her knees up to her chest, glaring at her guitar across the room.

Her first impulse, of course, was to pack up and leave. And maybe she should. Her cheeks were flaming with anger, and she couldn't remember when she had been so angry.

How dare he!

She tilted her head back and began to take several deep breaths to calm herself.

Count to a hundred, Robin, she said to herself. *Count slow and long before you do something you'll regret.*

Craig was out the back door and down the path to the barn, his head throbbing with anger, his heart pounding from the day's stress.

Who did she think she was to come in here and tell him what was wrong with his sons? And how could she know there was anything wrong when she'd only been here a short time? And just because Zack couldn't sit still when she read to him...

He walked into the barn and stopped, breathing deeply of the sweet hay. Slowly he walked past the bank of stalls to the last one, where Diamond was munching feed. The Palomino with a diamond-shaped blaze had not been well, and now as Craig unlatched the gate and entered, he decided to spoil Diamond a bit. He'd curry him, give him a sugar cube, be with an animal he loved.

"You'll be good as new, pal," he said, stroking his neck.

While he tried to concentrate on his work, something kept nagging him. Robin's words were a repetition of what that gal —Brianna Adams—had told him right before he left Omak. At the time, he had been certain Zack, like Will and himself, was suffering the aftermath of shock and grief over Brenda.

After he finished with the horse and put everything away. Then he turned and walked out to the corral, glancing at the house.

Zack was racing across the yard, leaping for the pass Will had thrown him. Suddenly tears clouded Craig's eyes, tears of love and worry and frustration. He wanted so much for his sons to have a good life, yet no matter how he had tried to protect them, they had already been exposed to a crushing heartbreak with the death of their mother, a change of schools, and a way of life that might not last much longer. The banker in Cranbrook had turned him down on a loan. He wasn't surprised, but he couldn't help feeling embarrassed and humiliated. He had spoken with optimism to Mr. Spencer about the ranch and his future, yet he had known the outcome was spelled out in black and white in the financial statement that lay on Doug Spencer's desk. And he hated it.

"The problem is," Spencer said, "cattle ranching is a gamble these days, even for those with years of experience."

Craig nodded. "But I'm raising horses, too," he reminded the banker.

"I wish I could help," Spencer came to his feet, "but I'm afraid the board wouldn't go along with this loan. The property has potential—I'm aware of that. I just don't think it has the potential to earn a living for you."

"We'll see," Craig had said, extending his hand. "Thank you for your time, Mr. Spencer."

"My pleasure. And say hello to Robin for us."

"I will."

On his way out, he glanced around the bank for Kathy, but she was out.

Now, as he thought about the events of the day, he knew he was already on his last nerve when Robin mentioned Zack's problem. He couldn't deal with that yet.

Well, there was one more bank left, one he hadn't hit for a loan. It was the large bank in Omak that had financed the ranch there. He didn't know what their policy was on loaning money for a ranch up in Canada, but it wouldn't hurt to ask. It was his last resort.

Robin came out the front door, her duffel bag in her arms, and suddenly everyone in the yard froze.

"Where are you going?" Zack demanded, making a dash toward her.

She glanced over his head to Craig, then took a deep breath, forcing a smile as Zack approached. "I really need to get back to Calgary and check on my mom's house. She's down in Florida and—"

"You can't go!" Will said firmly. He had reached her side now, slipping a hand in hers and tugging hard. "I wanted us to go up to Horsethief Park." He whirled around to face Craig, who was sheepishly making his way toward Robin. "Dad, you said that's where we could find the most arrowheads. Robin promised to go with me to find arrowheads."

Robin tilted her head and looked into his face. "Did I promise?"

When Will hesitated, Zack, who was not above lying, jumped in. "Yeah, you did; you promised. I heard you."

A little grin tugged at her lips as she looked over at Zack. "You heard me all the way down at the barn?"

"Dad," Will looked to him for help, "you said sometime we could go up to Horsethief Park to camp? Can we do that tonight?"

131

Craig took a deep breath. "Looks like she's leaving now," he said, as his eyes met hers. They stared at one another.

She took a deep breath, turning her gaze back to Zack. "I don't have to leave exactly now," she said, thrusting her chin out stubbornly and looking at Zack. "I never had a brother, you know. And my sisters were a couple of sissies. If you guys want me to go camping, I'll go." She looked back at Will. "After seeing your arrowhead collection, I'd like to help you find a few more."

Robin's kindness toward his boys knocked down Craig's barricade of anger. Slowly, he approached her, taking a deep breath, ready to eat crow.

"That is a very nice gesture on your part," he said. "And I appreciate it." He looked at the boys. "I was mean and short-tempered with Robin earlier. You guys need to understand, she's doing this for you."

"And for me," she answered.

"So can we go now?" Will pressed the point. He and Zack were already pulling her duffel bag out of her hands and holding on tight, as though she might change her mind.

"It's up to you," Craig said, looking at Robin.

"Well," she shrugged, "I haven't quit this job yet, though I have a feeling you'd like it if I did."

"No, he wouldn't," Will interceded.

"Why don't you guys go pack up your gear?" Craig suggested.

"We're going?" Will asked, grinning at Zack.

"Yep."

"I can manage the boys without you," Robin offered. "You don't have to go."

Will frowned. "Grizzlies might be up there."

"That's right," Craig answered quickly. "I can't let you three go alone. I'll go with you. Sam can finish up what I was doing at the corral."

Both boys gave a yelp of approval and tore out for the house. "I'll get the sleeping bags," Will called over his shoulder.

"There's an extra one on the top shelf of the back closet. Get that one for Robin." He glanced at her. "I bought a couple of new ones in case the boys take friends camping."

Shoving his hands in his pockets, he took a few steps closer. "Again, I want to say I appreciate you doing this for the boys. As for the things I said to you, go ahead and take a shot at me. I deserve it."

She squinted through the sunlight, appraising him thoughtfully.

His denim shirt and Levi's were clean, his boots neatly polished, yet he had a worn look about him, as though he felt exhausted. He stood tall and looked powerful, every inch the man who was in full control, yet she saw his humility and something more—a vulnerable quality that hadn't been there.

He was looking at her with that same kind of quiet pleading she often saw on Will's face, and she could feel herself caving in again. She also saw the weariness etched into every line of his face, and the dark shadows underneath his eyes.

"No, Craig, you don't deserve a shot of sarcasm," she said softly, wearied by the stress of their quarreling. "Hey, I know you have your problems here."

He looked at her curiously. Her tone was kind and understanding, and her eyes were gentle as she looked at him. Now he felt even worse about losing his temper with her. "I'm on edge, obviously, but I should never have blown up at you," he said quietly.

"Well, I fired right back, so I think we came out about even."

Craig looked her squarely in the eye and felt that stirring again in his heart. He hadn't wanted to feel anything for her, but that was becoming impossible. She was wearing a pale blue denim shirt that softened her hazel eyes and set off her red-gold hair. Her mouth was tilted in one of those little smiles he liked, yet this one was sad and a bit wistful.

"Well, if you aren't just being nice and you really want to go camping, I guess we'd better get ready. They certainly are," he inclined his head toward the house where the boys' voices were raised to fever pitch. Even the sounds of drawers slamming could be heard clearly.

"What do I need to get from the kitchen?" she asked, as they walked to the house.

"I keep a camp box ready in the pantry," he said. "It has cooking utensils, coffeepot, paper plates and cups, and a thermos for juice or milk. I'll get it."

"There's a pack of hot dogs in the fridge, and I picked up some marshmallows when I was in town." She smiled. "I had been planning a wiener roast."

"Great!" he grinned.

"I'll pack fruit and cheese, and peanut butter and jelly as well."

"We've had peanut butter and jelly sandwiches for breakfast many times," Craig said. "Don't forget to put in plenty of coffee."

They were both speaking in happy voices by the time they reached the house, and in record time everything was boxed up and they were all on their horses with both boys talking at once as they rode toward Horsethief Park.

Seventeen

They stopped for a break at Middle Meadow, where Clear Creek made a wide bend. There were several smooth rocks where they could sit and munch the apples Robin had packed. They even gave apples to the horses.

"I'll bet this place is a real picture in winter when snow covers everything," Robin said, looking around, refreshed and contented.

"Yeah, it's beautiful," Craig said, taking a last bite of his apple. "Okay, guys, lets give the horses a chance to get a drink."

They all led their horses to the creek, and stuck their hands into the refreshing water.

"Should we refill our canteens?" Will asked.

He and Zack had brought along their own little canteens attached to their belts. Robin could see this was a special trip for them, and they seemed to have thought of everything.

"Good idea." Craig glanced over their heads to Robin's eyes and exchanged amused grins with her. "But no drinking it until we have a chance to boil it. Even though it is so clear we shoudn't just drink it."

They mounted up again as the breeze slipped over the valley, gently rippling the meadow grass, soft as green silk.

"Bet the wind gets pretty fierce in the winter," Robin said as she and Craig rode stirrup to stirrup. The boys were just ahead, talking loudly about the possibility of seeing a grizzly.

"Yep. It can be a two-faced friend: kind and gentle one day, bitter and cruel the next."

She twisted in her saddle and looked at him. "Is there a message in that for me?"

He chuckled, looking across at her. "No. You aren't two-faced. And I certainly would never think of you as a monster. That idea is not original. It comes from a story I read the boys one evening."

"Oh."

Beneath Craig's tan Stetson, his dark eyes glowed, and his skin, bronzed from the sun, accented the brilliance of his white teeth. She tried to imagine the tough-looking man reading children's books. The vision tugged at her heart in such a strong way that she had to turn and gaze at a raven circling overhead.

There were so many things about Craig that she admired—his love and gentleness with his boys, his unselfishness on their behalf, his gentleness when someone needed him.

She chewed her lip, staring across at the woods where the pines grew taller, denser. If only he could adjust his attitude a bit, stop being so uptight, so rigid. Losing his wife had left a deep wound, yet he was reluctant to let anyone in to help him heal. She couldn't figure out why he was that way; he and the boys should be happy and relaxed in this tranquil setting.

Ahead, wildflowers dappled the meadow in rainbow colors as the sun began to drop toward the horizon, and the horses climbed the trail leading into Horsethief Park.

A squirrel scampered down a pine beside the trail, breaking the peaceful silence. Robin glanced at Zack and saw that he was completely still, perfectly content, not even fidgeting in the saddle.

She thought about what she had said to Craig, who was glancing at Zack as well. No doubt Craig was measuring his activity today and thinking that Robin was way off base about his son having attention deficit disorder. What Craig didn't understand was that Zack had found his element, here in the midst of nature while riding his favorite horse.

They had reached the top meadow, and below on their right she could see a corner of Skook's cabin. The patched roof had a red glow in the late afternoon sunshine, and she wondered how often Skook and Jenny had climbed the trail to picnic up here.

"Why is this called Horsethief Park?" she asked as they looked around for the perfect camp spot.

"It's a name often given to high, secluded meadows—comes from the old days of cattle rustlers. Horse thieves looked for a secret meadow to hide their stolen horses, a place that was easily guarded."

"Well, this is the place," she laughed lightly. "I hope there's no cattle rustling going on now," she joked.

He shook his head. "Nah, the name Horsethief Park is just a name used like beaver creek or trout creek. And speaking of beavers, we have them here." He motioned toward a small tributary of the creek where an animal had built a tiny dam.

"Hey, boys," he called, "this looks like a good spot. We're close enough to the creek to get water, yet we're out of the wind."

The boys hopped down, and everyone went to work setting up camp. Robin unpacked groceries while the boys and Craig went in search of firewood. Soon a crackling fire was going, and the wieners were roasting on sharpened willow sticks.

Will and Zack were careful with their sticks, mesmerized by the way the wieners roasted while their juice trickled down the sticks and exploded into the campfire.

Behind them, a blazing hot-pink sunset cast liquid fire into the beaver pond and warmed the aging pines.

As the four campers finished off their hotdogs and dug into the marshmallows, the sunset faded, leaving a blanket of gray across the sky. The cool night air surrounded them, and Craig went to dig out jackets for everyone. Robin was hovering closer to the fire until Craig wrapped one of his jackets around her.

Shivering into it, she smiled up at him. "Thanks."

"You're welcome. Boys," he turned back to them, "time to unroll our sleeping bags. We'll bunk down over there, and Robin can stay near the fire. You'll be warmer," he assured her.

She nodded, watching Zack and Will trudge off to the woods, then return to sit down on their sleeping bags, removing their shoes and dusting off their socks before climbing into the bags.

Craig walked back to join Robin on one of the logs they had pulled up to the fire.

"I thought we could talk for a few minutes, if you'd like to."

"Sure. I'm not real sleepy yet. Just contented," Robin said.

"So you think Zack has…" He frowned, stumbling for the term.

"ADD. Attention deficit disorder. Yes, I do. I can recognize it because I have it, too."

He stared at her, watching a little smile curl her mouth.

"And it hasn't stopped me from getting a good education or enjoying life. Maybe I enjoy life even more than some people because I have the ability to hyperfocus once my attention is centered. And that's the way it will be for Zack. This is not a learning disability, Craig. Honestly, many people who have this

138

are very smart; their smartness just gets tangled up at times."

Craig nodded, looking at her thoughtfully. "Can you help Zack with this?"

"He should be tested by someone who is qualified, and that person can make a recommendation. He may need some personal tutoring to get him back on track, and I can do that while I'm here. I think if we put a horse in every project, he would come through with flying colors!"

Craig grinned. "No doubt."

"Also, motivating him is very important. I've been told that in situations where a person is highly motivated, the symptoms of ADD can disappear. I saw an example of that with a student of mine who was a gymnast."

Craig looked at her for a moment, saying nothing as his eyes examined her face, lingered on her lips, then returned to her eyes.

"I want to explain why I was so edgy today," he said, glancing across at his sleeping sons. "This morning I went into Cranbrook and asked your uncle—however many times removed—for a loan. He turned me down."

"He did what?"

Craig put a finger to his lips, signalling her to lower her voice.

She leaned closer to Craig, trying to calm her temper but feeling a rush of anger. Why couldn't Uncle Doug see the potential Craig had? "He made a mistake—"

"No, he made a sound business decision," Craig said wearily. "As much as I hate to admit it, I'm not a bankable asset right now, Robin. To tell you the truth, I didn't expect to get the loan. After all, my track record in the cattle business doesn't look good."

"I can't believe he turned you down," she said, staring

blankly into the campfire, still stunned by this news. "Sundance should have some sentimental value for him; after all, his great-uncle—I think that's right—homesteaded it."

"Then maybe he would like to buy it," Craig said dryly.

"No, he doesn't want it," Robin sighed. "He wasn't at all interested in the ranch, not when I spoke to him."

"Not everyone wants to be a rancher."

She turned and looked at him. "There must be a way. Don't give up, Craig."

He reached across and took her hand, and automatically she laced her fingers through his. "Thanks for the encouragement," he said, pulling her gently toward him.

His lips were warm in the cool night as he kissed her. With the firelight creating a mellow glow around them and the boys snoring contentedly in the background, Robin realized how happy she was with Craig and the boys. If only Uncle Doug had not turned him down on the loan!

One of the boys was coughing, and slowly Craig pulled back from her. "I'll never live it down if one of the boys looks over and catches Dad smooching in the moonlight!"

Robin smiled into his eyes, then glanced over at the two small bundles. One was wiggling.

"We'd better say good night."

"I know. So good night." He gave her another quick kiss, then got up to check her sleeping bag one last time. "Sure you'll be okay?" he asked, smoothing a strand of hair back from her face.

"I'll be fine," she said. "I'm a seasoned camper, so you don't have to worry about me."

"That's good to know." Still he lingered, as though he really hated to say good night.

"Dad?" A muffled voice floated into the darkness.

"Time to get to your side of the fire," she teased.

Slipping off her boots, she snuggled down into the sleeping bag and looked up at the sky. To her right, dark pines spiraled into the darkness, and beyond that, silver moonlight flooded the mountain peaks. She heard Craig whispering to one of the boys, and then there was a rustling of sleeping bags. She imagined him taking off his boots, crawling down into the sleeping bag beside his sons.

Then there was only the sound of gentle breathing, a crackling fire, and the flapping of a beaver's tail against the water. She closed her eyes and took a deep, pine-scented breath.

Thank you, God, for the privilege of being here.

Craig awakened at daylight and crawled out of his sleeping bag before the others awoke. He wanted to punch up the fire and get some fresh water from the creek.

As he pulled on his boots and windbreaker, his eyes shot eagerly to Robin's sleeping bag. All he could see was the top of her red hair as she snuggled into the warmth of the down-filled bag.

He took a deep breath and forced himself to continue with his mission rather than stand there, staring at her.

Her encouragement had given him the extra boost he needed, and now he found new hope running through his heart, as persistent as the creek chattering over the stones. As he walked toward the creek, he made a decision. He had one alternative left, and he was going to make the most of it. He would call his banker in Omak and try to get a loan. Perhaps the banker would have a suggestion on the best way to handle the matter. The worst he could do was say no, so Craig had nothing to lose by asking. Nothing but his pride, and that was becoming excess baggage.

Eighteen

❧

They spent an hour searching for arrowheads and found only one, but Will was thrilled with it. Then they saddled up and headed home.

As soon as they arrived at the house, Craig made a quick excuse to go into town. Leaving Robin in charge of the boys and lunch, he drove breakneck to use the telephone in town, placing a call to Omak.

Half an hour later, he was headed home again, feeling worse than before. He'd been wrong about having nothing to lose by hearing another "Sorry, Craig, but..."

While the Omak banker sounded sincerely regretful, it was against their policy to make loans outside the United States. And no, there was no other angle to take, since the property to be financed was in Canada.

Craig's high hopes had crashed by the time he hung up the phone and dragged himself back to the truck. It was getting more and more difficult to pull his heart out of his boots. He had to let go of this fantasy about a loan, he told himself rationally. He had to accept reality.

As he turned into the driveway and saw the boys out in the

yard playing football, his heart sank lower, if that was possible. He knew what losing the ranch would do to them, but it was out of his hands now. He had done everything he could to hold on.

He parked the truck and cut the engine, dragging himself out. As he slowly approached the yard, he thought of his neighbor, Tom Walton. Tom had told him he would be interested in buying Craig's property if he ever decided to sell. But Craig knew Walton wouldn't pay him what it was worth.

He and Sam had been working on fences and outbuildings, hoping to make a profit when and if he sold the ranch. But he was running out of time.

He approached Will as he made a long pass to Zack, then turned to his father for approval.

"Very good," Craig said, clamping a hand on Will's shoulder. "I have to go over to the Waltons for a little while. Think you guys can hold it down for the next hour?"

"Can we go with you?" Zack yelled

"Not this time."

"But—"

Craig put up his hand, cutting off the objections spilling from Zack's lips. "Not this time," he repeated firmly. "I want to talk business with Mr. Walton. If you guys get hungry—" he broke off, glancing back at the house.

He wondered if he should go in and discuss this with Robin. No, she would try to talk him out of selling the ranch, but it was his decision. And he knew what he must do, whether he wanted to or not.

"Don't you guys get too rough on your tackling while I'm gone," he said, heading for his pickup as the boys returned to their football game.

He had to think of what was best for them, he told himself. And with that uppermost in his mind, he drove toward the

Walton ranch, ready to talk terms.

And maybe tonight he'd swallow that lump of pride in his throat, force himself to write to his father-in-law, and accept his offer of a job in the lumber business.

There were some advantages to the arrangement, he told himself, although at the moment he couldn't seem to think of any.

Nineteen

I s it true?" Will burst out at the dinner table.

Robin's head popped up from the baked chicken. She looked curiously at Will.

At the opposite end of the table, Craig looked from Will to Zack, then back at Will. "Who were you talking with on the cell-phone just now?" Craig asked.

Will's face was flushed with anger, and his dark eyes blazed. "I was talking with Jimmy Walton. He said his grandfather is buying our ranch!"

Craig slumped in the chair, feeling as though a fist had just plowed into his stomach. Never had he wanted the news to come out like this, especially not from someone other than himself, someone like the Walton boy who enjoyed taunting Will.

"Mr. Walton made me an offer," he said, looking Will squarely in the eye. He had always been honest with his sons. "I haven't accepted the offer, but—"

"Then why would Jimmy say that?" Will asked, looking relieved.

Craig sighed. "Because I agreed to think about it."

Zack's fork clanged loudly on the plate. "I'm not gonna go live with Grandma!" He leaped from his chair and bolted down the hall to his room, punctuating his departure with a fierce slam of the door.

Craig was glad that Robin sat in her chair, her eyes on her salad. This was none of her business, and Craig didn't want her involved in a family row. Yet she was. He couldn't help recalling what he had told her on their horseback ride and the sympathy on her face when he spoke of his problems in trying to make the ranch a financial success.

"Aren't you gonna make him come back and eat?" Will demanded. "He can act any way he wants to and he never gets punished."

"I'm not going to force him to eat when he's upset, Will. I've never demanded that of you and I've certainly never punished you for it."

Will slumped forward, staring at his glass of milk. "Why are you even thinking about letting Mr. Walton buy this ranch?"

Craig saw Robin staring at him, waiting for an answer. He frowned at Will. "Stop badgering me!"

"But he has a right to know," Robin said, then put one hand to her mouth with a stricken look, as if she'd been unable to stop herself from speaking.

"Excuse me," he snapped, "but I don't think this concerns you."

"No," she said coolly, "I guess not." She folded her napkin and stood up. "Excuse *me*."

Will watched her as she left the kitchen by the back door while Craig sat staring glumly into his plate. He had done it again, but why couldn't she see it was difficult enough to explain matters to the boys? She merely added to the frustration when she challenged him, too.

He took a deep breath, trying to compose himself. He was glad she had chosen to excuse herself. It was bad enough to try to explain his actions to his son; it was even worse with a stranger sitting in.

Robin wasn't a stranger, he reminded himself. No matter how he tried to keep his relationship with her casual, he was starting to have feelings for her. He knew that, and it scared him.

He also knew how she felt about this ranch, which brought him back to the memory of that conversation with her distant uncle.

"Look, Will," Craig finally said, "I've spoken with two different bankers about operating loans." He hesitated, hating to admit the truth, but he hated even more trying to hide things from his sons. "I can't get a loan. Unless I figure out a way to make more money on the ranch, I may have to...think of something else. Since our land adjoins Mr. Walton's, he's always been interested in it. I just needed to know if what he would offer was even worth considering. That's all that's happened."

"I'm not hungry," Will grumbled, pushing aside his plate and coming to his feet. He dashed off down the hall to join Zack.

Craig sat at the table and stared aimlessly at the food, hardly touched. How could he make them understand? How could he accept this himself?

He sat pondering what to do. He had tried to think of everything, yet he seemed to be getting nowhere.

Robin strolled through the soft darkness, staring up at the starry sky, enjoying the feel of the night wind on her face. In the distance, she could see the mountains etched against the sky. She took a deep breath of the pine-scented air and tried to relax. It was so beautiful here. If only she had the money to buy the land. For one insane moment, she even considered asking Craig how much he wanted for his ranch, then quickly dismissed her idea as absurd.

She did well to balance her budget and make her car payment. Yet...

Her eyes lingered on the mountains as she chewed the corner of her lip. She had never done well at saving her money, so for the past three years she had invested a small portion of her salary in a CD account. She had built up a tiny nest egg, but she doubted that her savings would even buy an acre of Sundance. She followed the path to the pasture fence and stood staring at the dark forms of the horses grazing.

Her mind drifted back to the day before, the wonderful afternoon she had spent with Craig. He had been kind and gentle and considerate, but today the old Craig was back, gruff and explosive.

Sugar had wandered up to the fence, and she reached out, stroking his forehead.

"You're a sweetie," she said. "Too bad your master is such an old grouch."

"An old grouch, huh?"

She whirled around, startling Sugar. She hadn't heard Craig walk up behind her.

"You frightened me!" she snapped, turning back to watch Sugar trot out to pasture again.

A night wind blew softly over Sundance Ranch, and from the corral a horse neighed. Robin loved it here, but she had to leave. And she had to tell Craig.

The moonlight filtered down over her face as she turned to him. He was looking into her eyes, shaking his head.

"You just don't understand," he said.

"You're right. I don't understand you at all. How can you be so kind and sensitive one minute and so gruff and uncaring the next?"

"I don't mean to be gruff." His voice was as soft as the breeze caressing her face. He seemed so different from the man who had rebuffed her earlier. "And I'm certainly not uncaring..."

He dipped his head to kiss her lips, and Robin felt torn with frustration and uncertainty. Who was Craig Cameron? She wasn't sure. Yet she was sure of one thing: she was falling in love with him, and she couldn't seem to stop herself.

She tore her lips from his. The anger had melted away, and that was not good, she decided, trying to hold on to it as a defense against his persuasiveness.

"I'm going back to the house," she said, turning and setting off up the path to the back door.

Much, much later she heard his footsteps in the hallway past her door. Once again, they had avoided one another. He had remained in his office until late. The boys had no interest in playing games with her, and she was glad. She wanted to be alone. She had insisted she must write some letters tonight and had gone to her room and closed the door.

Later, she heard Craig talking with the boys in the living room. *Fine, let them be a family again.* Without her in the way.

She knew she should leave, and she told herself she would in the morning. But as she lay in the darkness of her bedroom, staring out at the night sky, she knew it would be hard to leave the ranch. It would be even harder to say good-bye to Craig and the boys.

The sound of feet racing down the hall the next morning

woke her. The boys' voices echoed from the kitchen, mingling with a deeper voice. Not Craig's, but another's. She peered at the clock and saw it was after eight. Everyone was up but her.

Quickly, she grabbed her robe and slippers and dashed across to the bathroom to tidy up. Along the way, the deep voice of a stranger reached her.

"It's the truth, the absolute truth!"

At that, she could hear the boys' laughter, and she realized someone was entertaining them in the kitchen.

Hurrying through her morning rituals, she quickly pulled on her jeans and a T-shirt and wandered toward the kitchen to see what was going on.

The boys were seated at the table, eating cereal. Craig was draining the coffeepot, refilling the mug of a strange-looking little man.

"Harley's come home!" Zack announced proudly.

Robin's eyes turned to the man, who looked as though he had ridden some rough trails in his time. Craig was introducing her to him, and she made the appropriate response as she stood looking at Harley, totally fascinated.

He stood five feet six inches, no more than one hundred and forty pounds, she guessed. Yet his slender build was well muscled. She guessed he was middle-aged, but it was difficult to tell. Robin suspected the weathered lines in his face had come early.

He was wearing a pair of brown jeans, and a faded, blue-and-gray, long-sleeved western shirt. His cowboy hat in early years might have been brown, but she couldn't be sure about the color now. She tried to hold back an amused grin as she studied the ill-shaped hat. It looked as though an elephant had slept on it.

In a long thin face, his eyes were a merry blue, holding a twinkle that seemed to match the one in Zack's eyes. She could see they would be a good pair.

"It's nice to meet you, Harley," Robin said, accepting a cup of coffee from Craig.

"You, too, ma'am." He remembered his hat and yanked it off, unsettling a few strands of thinning gray hair.

"She's a good cook, but she doesn't know much about rodeoing," Zack announced.

"And just how do you know I don't?" she challenged him. "Want to have a race sometime?"

"No, he doesn't," Craig spoke up.

Harley chuckled as his eyes lingered for a moment on Robin. She could see he was sizing her up before he turned back to the boys. "Okay, you two, finish up your breakfast and come on down to the bunkhouse with me. I've brought you back a little souvenir from town."

"How does your leg feel?" Craig asked, looking concerned.

"Ready to take on a bucking horse! Since I got the cast off, I can outrun Zack if I need to."

Everyone laughed as the boys gulped down the last of their cereal, then bounded out the door with Harley for the bunkhouse.

Robin and Craig sat for a moment in awkward silence.

"They're glad to see Harley," she said, trying to make conversation with Craig as he put away the milk.

"Yeah. He's just as much a kid at heart as they are. They have a lot of fun together." His eyes drifted to her, and she tilted her head and looked at him.

"Craig, what are you going to do? About the ranch, I mean."

He took a deep breath. "I'm not sure. Frankly, I don't like cattle ranching that much anyway."

She leaned forward, searching his face. "What would you really want to do?"

His eyes drifted toward the window, staring off into the distance. "I guess I like the idea of being a rancher more than I like

151

ranching. In Omak I made a decent living with quarter horses, but now I don't have the capital for a horse breeding ranch."

"If you had the capital, is that what you'd do?"

"Maybe." He looked back at her and sighed. "Robin, I have to think of the boys. The most sensible plan is to sell out and go back to the States. I know I can make a decent living for us down there. I'll think of something." He looked at her with a sad smile.

"You've been great to the boys." Craig hesitated, then seemed to swallow the rest of his pride. "And I appreciate your kindness to me. Even when I don't deserve it."

"I happen to think you deserve it."

His eyes lingered on her uptilted face as she sat very still, watching him. She let her expression show that she cared about him and the boys and what happened to them, and she could see he was touched.

Craig stood and walked around the table to her chair, smiling down at her. "You're a wonderful person," he said, reaching for her hand. "Thanks for being honest with me about Zack. I'm relieved to know he's not a slow learner as his last teacher suggested."

"No, he's very bright. You know that."

"Yeah. And you've been very patient with him...and with me." He lifted her hand to his lips, kissing it gently. "Honestly, I don't know how you put up with us. Sometimes we're a pretty sorry lot."

"Not sorry, just stubborn," she said teasingly. "And endowed with a strong dose of pride."

He chuckled.

"And am I that patient?" she laughed. "I believe you got a preview of my famous temper. You know it comes with being a redhead."

Craig grinned, lifting a hand to touch a soft strand of her thick hair. "You have beautiful hair. It was one of the first things I admired about you."

"I guess men either like it or they don't like it. There doesn't seem to be any alternative."

Craig glanced through the screen door to the bunkhouse. "Robin, now that Harley has come home, why don't I ask him to watch the boys this afternoon? I'd like to take you someplace special for an early dinner."

Robin glanced in the direction of the bunkhouse where shouts of laughter could be heard. The boys were having a great time with Harley.

"Okay, if you want to."

"Today we're going to put up some fence," he continued, "but I'll knock off early and we'll drive in about four o'clock if that suits you."

"Sure, Craig. By the way, since Harley is back, I guess I'll be going."

He frowned. "No, I need you to stay on at least another week."

"But why?"

"To help out with the boys. And keep up the cooking too, if you don't mind. Sam and I need Harley to help us on the fence. And we want to patch up the roof on the barn. Is that okay?"

Robin shrugged. "Sure. Then maybe I should do some grocery shopping while we're in town."

"Fine. I'd like to take you to Stagshead to eat, then afterward we can go to the grocery store in Fort Steele."

She tilted her head and looked up at him. "Are you sure you need me to stay on?"

He reached for her hand. "I really, really need you."

Twenty

❦

The day passed quickly. For lunch, Robin whipped up a stir-fry meal using the raw vegetables in the refrigerator and adding tiny pieces of sirloin from a chunk she had located in the freezer. She wished for her wok and her special stir-fry sauce, but she made do with some soy sauce in the cabinet and the spices she had brought along with her. She served it on a bed of rice, prepared from the huge supply Craig kept in the cabinet.

Harley had raved over her food, not seeming the least bit jealous that he had been temporarily replaced in the kitchen. Craig and the boys cleaned up their plates, and then the boys reminded Harley about that new Chinese checkers game he had brought back, and they were off to the bunkhouse again.

That evening, as they sat in the dining room of the Stagshead, Robin and Craig relaxed and discussed the events of the day.

"I'm glad you suggested coming here," Robin said, admiring the restaurant. Cathedral ceilings opened up the room, and log walls held a variety of western art. Their table overlooked a small blue lake.

"It's a bit rustic, but I think the food is terrific. And the view is nice," he added, glancing from the lake back to Robin.

Their eyes locked for a moment, then the waiter appeared with menus and Craig glanced around the room. "They have a great buffet dinner. Want to try it?"

"Sure!" She thought about how easy it was to agree on everything this evening. Being away from the ranch seemed to have erased the cares for a while.

After they had loaded up a couple of plates and returned to the table, the waiter poured tall glasses of iced tea, then left them to enjoy their meal.

"Mmm, best homemade bread I've tasted since Mom baked bread," Robin said, munching a thick crusty roll.

"I'll bet your mother is a good cook."

"She is. I've kept a copy of her best recipes. She taught me everything I know about the kitchen."

"Well, she taught you well," he replied. "I'm enjoying your cooking, and I can't help noticing," he grinned at her, "that you favor baking over frying and stir-frying over boiling. It tastes good the way you prepare it."

She smiled. "The seasonings I put in have a lot to do with enhancing the flavor of the food."

"I didn't think we had much variety in the cabinet."

"I bought some spices when I went grocery shopping. I only wish I had brought my wok. I have a special Chinese dish that I enjoy preparing."

"I'd be glad to buy a wok for the kitchen if you need one."

"That's okay. I have enough other recipes to keep me busy." She looked away to her tea. She couldn't help wondering if she would be there long enough to break in a new wok. When she glanced at Craig, he seemed to be reading her mind.

"Even if I have to sell the ranch, life wouldn't be so bad if I saw you occasionally."

She buttered a roll and tried to choose her words carefully. "Depends on where you'll be, Craig. I have to tell you, I'm not crazy about cities. Calgary is big, but we live out in a small community. Can you believe I lived in LA for a year? Couldn't wait to get out. Then I went almost as far as I could in the opposite direction. A small town in Maine. I liked New England, but I still had wanderlust in my soul. So I headed south the next summer, applied for a job in Charleston, and got it."

"I'm guessing you couldn't wait to leave again."

"You got it. Only this time I came home. I want to stay in Canada, Craig."

He nodded, taking the last bite and pushing his plate aside. "So do I." He turned to stare at the lake.

"Tell me about your life," Robin said, wanting to keep the mood pleasant. "Did you grow up in Seattle?"

"In a suburb. I don't like cities either. When I was thirteen, I got a job working for a man who raised quarter horses. I remember Mom used to drive me ten miles out to his place every day after school. I think she and Dad both knew I'd found something I really wanted to do."

"You like horses a lot?"

"And everything connected with them. I didn't even mind shoveling out the manure just to be near those horses."

She smiled. "Your parents must be very understanding people."

"They are. They've always struggled, but we had a happy home, and they have a good marriage. Dad worked for a construction company, and Mom worked part-time as a secretary. She wanted to be at home with us as much as possible when we were growing up. Dad retired three years ago, and they sold their house and bought some land in the country. They're living in a mobile home while they build their dream house. They're

156

actually doing most of the work themselves."

"Really? Mom and Dad did some of the work on our home in Calgary."

"Dad's subcontracting the plumbing and wiring, but he and Mom are doing the painting and wallpapering. He's building the cabinets. They're doing a good job and having fun in the process."

"I guess your parents miss Zack and Will."

"They do, although they have other grandchildren in the area. Of course they'd like to see us more often, but they want me to be happy. And they believe the ranch makes me happy. Mom came up to help us get settled in, then Dad came to pick her up, and they stayed on for another week."

"They sound like very nice people."

"They are. I wish you could meet them. And I'd really like for them to meet you."

The waiter reappeared, and they both declined dessert but ordered coffee. The sun was setting over the lake, and Robin thought how peaceful her afternoon with Craig had been. She loved talking to him when he was relaxed and willing to communicate with her about himself and his family.

"Brenda and I married young," he said, startling her with this bit of news.

"Oh?" She wanted to know about his first wife but was reluctant to ask any questions.

"We dated through high school and got married the summer after we graduated. Her parents really wanted us to wait, but we were headstrong. We agreed to go on to college, but then Will was born the following year."

Craig took a deep breath, looking out at the lake. "I was too proud to take money from her parents, so I held down a full-time job and went to school at night. It took me five and a half years to get through college but I guess that's okay, considering I had a wife and two sons to support."

"You were in Seattle during this time?"

He nodded. "I earned a degree in business, so I went to work as a salesman for a chemical company. I hated it."

"How did you end up in Omak?"

"Remember I told you I got a part-time job for a man who raised horses back in junior high? Well, I kept up my friendship with him. I took the boys out to visit practically every weekend. We helped him out for the pleasure of being there. He offered to sell me a few acres of land next to his for a price I could afford. I bought it and then hit a lucky streak. A bypass was put in the next year, and my property was bought for five times what I paid for it. With that money, we moved to Omak and made a down payment on a small place and went into the business of raising quarter horses."

He looked down at his coffee, saying nothing for several seconds. Robin averted her eyes, thinking he was probably having some sad thoughts. She recalled he had told her that soon after he moved to Omak, tragedy struck Brenda.

"So, you and the boys came to British Columbia to get a fresh start," she said.

"Right." The waiter had brought the check, and Craig nodded, reaching for his billfold. "Well," he glanced at her, "I hate to leave, but I promised Harley we'd get back early. And we need to allow some time to pick up those groceries."

"Right. I'm ready to go."

As they left the restaurant, he reached out and grasped her hand. "You know, it feels good to hold hands with you, kinda like we're young and foolish."

"We are young and foolish," she said, tilting her head to look up with a mischievous smile. "We're as young as we want to be."

"You're much younger than I am."

"Twenty-six."

"And I'm twenty-nine."

"My dad once told me nothing really important happens until you're thirty. That it takes that long to grow up. But I think he was referring to the three girls he raised."

They had reached the car, and as he opened the door for her, he grinned. "So I'm out with a juvenile?"

"Not really."

They drove to the grocery store, and Craig grabbed a cart, pushing it along for her as she walked around the store. Occasionally, someone passed them and stopped to speak to Craig while Robin moved on, quickly locating the items she needed.

Ten sacks later, they were back in the truck, heading home. A contented silence flowed between them, and Robin felt no need to talk. She was happy just to look out at the peaceful farm houses they passed, seeing children playing in the yard or horses grazing in a distant meadow in the soft twilight. Above the valley floor, the mountains kept a watchful eye.

As Craig turned onto Sundance Road, Robin's eyes followed the curve of the landscape: the way the cottonwoods and willows at the creekbank outlined the meadow, the mountain straight ahead.

"The road looks as though it will dead-end into that mountain," Robin said, leaning her head back against the seat.

"Yeah, when I first drove in here, I liked the idea of being enclosed in our own private world." Craig, too, was gazing at the landscape, his arm resting lightly on the steering wheel.

It was a nice thought, Robin decided, trying not to think about the possibility of staying here. Yet she couldn't help herself.

Craig turned in at the road leading to the ranch, and Robin looked at the huge sign.

"That's a beautiful sign. Did you put it up?"

"No, one of the previous owners did it."

The sign was hung with three chains on either side between two posts, about twenty inches in diameter, towering at least ten feet high. It simply said: SUNDANCE, with the brand beside it.

"The brand, you know, is for Skook and Chuck," she smiled at him, grateful for all the knowledge she had of the ranch. Little had she known the years of hearing Granny's stories would someday be so useful to her.

"You know," he said, reaching across to squeeze her hand, "in the beginning I was a little envious that you knew so much about this place. Now, I'm grateful that you do. It gives me a special bond with you, as though someone cares about Sundance just half as much as I do."

She nodded slowly, thinking she cared about the ranch, and its present owner as well. For years she had felt a restlessness she could never quite define. That feeling was gone now, and she couldn't imagine having it return. But then, she was an adventurous spirit, never putting down roots for long.

This time it just might be different. For the first time, she really began to wish for a future with Craig. She knew she was in love with him, and she could only hope from the look in his eyes, from his words and his gestures, that he felt the same way about her. She wanted him to—more than she had ever wanted anything in her life.

I'm going to have to do some serious praying, she thought, as he turned into the driveway and they both looked to the wide porch where Harley sat, smoking his pipe, staring up at the sky.

"You two have a good evening?" he called, as they got out of the truck, picked up armloads of groceries, and walked up the porch steps.

"A very good evening," Craig answered. "Did the boys give you a hard time?"

"Nah, those boys know how to get along with me. Well," he pulled his wiry little frame up and started down the steps, "guess I'll go down and jaw with Sam for a while. Good night."

After the groceries had been put away, Craig turned back to her. "Want to sit on the porch for a while?"

"For just a minute," she said, leading the way out and dropping into the rocker with her feet tucked under her.

The days were long now, with daylight stretching past nine o'clock, but darkness had finally settled in with the pleasant night sounds that were a part of Sundance. Robin sighed. She kept thinking about Craig and the boys and wondering what they would do.

"Why the serious face?" Craig asked, looking across at her. The lights from the living room spilled onto the porch, bathing their faces in a golden glow.

"I don't know," she answered. "Well, maybe I do. I think I need some time to think. And to pray."

"That's what works for you, huh?"

"Praying? Yes. It works for me."

He shifted in his chair to stare out into the darkness. "It hasn't worked very well for me."

"Maybe there's a reason."

Craig looked across at her, his expression cynical. "What do you suppose the reason could be?"

She leaned forward, her eyes pulling at his, begging him to listen, to understand. "Craig, if you're meant to keep Sundance, and I believe that you are, there has to be a way to work things out. Remember Jenny Russell's verse…'No good thing does he withhold from those who walk uprightly.'"

"Maybe that's the catch," he said, leaning his head against the rocker and staring up at the sky. "My walk through life hasn't always been…upright. What do you think that means, anyway?"

Robin followed his eyes to the starry sky, searching for the right words. "I think walking uprightly means a person who tries to keep the Ten Commandments and live honorably. You are a believer, aren't you, Craig?"

"Of course. But..." he paused, shaking his head. "I break commandments on a regular basis."

"Who have you killed or stolen from?" she smiled gently.

He looked startled at first, then he grinned. "I seem to remember a commandment about having no idols. Maybe I've made this ranch a god."

"Maybe you have. But it's not too late to try and live up to that verse."

He met her eyes and took a deep breath, as though mulling over the idea.

"Craig, I think you're a very honorable person," Robin continued. "From what I've observed, you treat people fairly, you try to live by the Golden Rule, and you don't go around breaking commandments. Maybe you just need to turn everything over to God."

A sad expression touched his eyes. "Including myself?"

"Including yourself." She said nothing more as his eyes rose above her head, staring into space. She knew he was thinking about that. She also knew this was something Craig would have to work through on his own and in his own way. She couldn't push him.

"Dad!" Will called from the depths of the house.

"Guess I should go in and tell him good night. In some ways, Will seems to need me more than Zack."

"I understand that. Will seems to hold his feelings inside."

"He does. He was very close to his mother. Her death has left a terrible scar on his little heart."

"Then go to him. Thanks for a lovely evening."

He lingered at the door. "Want some coffee or hot chocolate

after I settle Will down?" he asked.

"No, thanks. I'm pretty tired." She stood up and walked toward the front door.

"Wait." He reached for her hand and pulled her gently to his side. "I don't know how to thank you for all you've done. You're changing my life. I feel it happening every day."

She tilted her head back to look up into his face and saw a gentleness in his dark eyes that almost took her breath away.

"I hope I've helped, Craig. But never forget one thing. No one can change you but God—and I think he's at work," she said, tiptoeing up to press a kiss on his cheek.

Twenty-One

After spending half an hour with Will, Craig crept past Robin's closed door and walked back to the porch. He sat down in the rocker where she had sat and talked to him about her faith. It had stirred him in a strange way. He was getting that same feeling he had experienced on Sunday when she'd strummed the guitar and everyone had sung "What a Friend We Have in Jesus."

He had voiced the words easily, naturally, for he had been raised in a church. In fact, he had met Brenda when she started attending his church during their freshman year in high school.

When had he started to stray off on his own, doing things his way, making his own decisions without praying about them?

He got up and started to walk, a restlessness sweeping over him. As he walked across the yard, the soft darkness around him, he began to wonder if there was a way to hang on to the ranch. His father-in-law had finally pulled out the big gun in yesterday's letter, making him an offer that would be difficult to refuse.

"Take over the family business in Seattle," he wrote. "By

doing this, you can ensure your future and have the security you need for Will and Zack. Also, they'll get plenty of tender loving care from Grandma and Grandpa."

He had hinted at that offer once before, but Craig had reminded him that he knew nothing about running a lumber company.

"I know," Frank had said, "but you're bright, ambitious; you can do the job. I'll train you myself."

Craig had appreciated the offer and promised to think it over, but he knew in his heart such a step would be wrong for him, personally. And yet it would ensure the boys' future.

Provided the boys *wanted* that kind of future.

Shoving his hands in his back pockets, he tilted his head back and shot his gaze heavenward.

"They're just like me," he said quietly. "They want to stay here." He bit his lip and looked around nervously.

I must be losing it, he thought. Here he was, standing in the middle of the yard, talking to himself. But the lights were out in the bunkhouse and the main house. Robin and the boys were asleep by now.

"All right, God," he whispered, "I'll do my best to walk...uprightly. Just please show me how to hang on to Sundance."

Robin woke with a new surge of energy. She sat up in bed and looked out the window, catching her breath at the glorious Canadian sunrise. It was still very early. Had a noise in the house awakened her? She strained her ears but heard nothing. Glancing at her bedside clock, she saw it was not yet six.

What on earth had happened to her? She never woke this early, yet here she was wide awake! So she might as well get out of bed and start the coffee. That led her thoughts toward Craig.

She sniffed for the smell of coffee lingering in the air. There was none. Was he already gone? Or had he overslept?

Walking over to the window, she pulled the drape back to look at the daylight breaking over the land. Down at the barn she could see Harley out poking around, a coffee mug in his hand. Her eyes moved on over the landscape, taking everything in, and she felt the sting of tears.

She hated to see Sundance sold again. She knew Jenny and Skook would like the idea of Craig and his sons starting over here. Through the blur of tears, her gaze moved slowly over the scene before her: grassy meadows, the horses grazing, the silver creek tumbling past the cottonwoods, and the mountains hemming the far end of the valley.

"There has to be a way," she said, feeling the trickle of tears on her cheeks. Several times she had fought the urge to go to town and phone Kathy, beg her to intercede with her father. But she knew Craig would not want that, and what good would Robin's plea do, anyway?

The land was beautiful, but Craig had said the growing seasons were too short for a cattle operation. And he didn't have the money to go back into raising quarter horses.

Her eyes lifted to the long streaks of crimson in the east where day was breaking. It was so beautiful here. If other people could come and enjoy it as she had, someone would give him a loan. *If other people could come and enjoy it...* Suddenly those words grew bolder in her mind, dominating her thoughts. Her eyes widened on the landscape. That was it!

Her brain was spinning with ideas and plans by the time she finished her shower, dressed, and entered the kitchen. Craig sat at the table, looking sleepy-eyed as he sipped his coffee. He was wearing a T-shirt and jeans, and he seemed in no hurry to get on with his chores for a change.

"Hi," she called to him.

"Hi. I hope you slept better than I did—"

"Craig, I just had a brainstorm," she said, reaching for a mug and pouring herself a cup of the strong brew. "I have to stop drinking this stuff," she mumbled, filling the mug.

"Does your brainstorm have something to do with the coffee?"

"Craig," she said, taking a seat at the table, "have you ever thought about using Sundance as a model for an authentic frontier ranch? Not in the sense of lodgers so much as offering trail rides and chuck wagon suppers and campfire sing-alongs?"

For a moment he looked dumbfounded, and she wondered if he thought her idea was crazy.

"Let me finish," she rushed on. "I learned something important when I taught down in the States. People are craving wholesome getaways, places to take their families to enjoy nature. You could buy a few more horses; you could even offer tent camping up at Middle Meadow. And the old cabin…" She paused, taking a sip of coffee and burning her tongue, but she scarcely noticed.

Craig had leaned forward on his elbows, watching her face intently.

"The Russell cabin. Craig, I want to hold onto that, even if I have to buy that from you or whoever lives here. You see, I'm not very good at managing money, so I arranged to have a small portion of my monthly check funneled into a savings account every month. After three years, I should have about—" She glanced at the ceiling, trying to figure it up. "About three thousand dollars."

Craig had tilted his head to the side, looking at her with an expression of amusement.

"I know, that won't even buy an acre here. But it would pay for some lumber and paint to fix up the cabin. And Craig, I would be willing to rent the cabin out to overnighters. Wouldn't it be neat to offer a packhorse trip up to the cabin, then furnish the supplies for a cookout and let the people do it themselves and stay in the cabin?"

Her hazel eyes were dancing and Craig stared at her, thunderstruck by her idea.

"That's incredible," he finally managed to respond. "You know, when I first came here it was as though I'd found the perfect hideaway from the world. I wouldn't have wanted to share it with anyone. But I've enjoyed having guests and seeing other people have a good time."

"See what I mean? And you're a good cook, Craig; with Harley's help, you could manage a great chuck wagon supper. And it would be so much fun!"

"Fun," he agreed, "but you're talking about summer trade. Unless—" He looked up at her. "I could give horseback riding lessons. I did that in Omak. And I could enlarge the barn a bit — maybe Sam and I could even build another one. Then I could board horses for extra income."

Craig leaned back in his chair. He looked as though he couldn't believe what he was hearing or how much sense it made.

"You know, Robin, there was a ranch out of Omak that catered to the tourist business. It wasn't a dude ranch, but rather a working ranch where people came and stayed to get in on roundups. The place did very well. I could call and get some ideas. Maybe make a trip down there."

She had reached across, touching his hand. "Craig, give it a try at least. Don't give up. Not yet."

He lifted her hand to his lips, kissing every finger. "Thanks to you, I won't."

They stared at one another for several seconds, then she gently withdrew her hand.

"I don't want you to think I'm trying to barge my way into all of this. It would be purely a business arrangement. I'm willing to make a stake in the cabin for sentimental reasons. And I'll do as much physical labor as I can. Then you can simply give me a tiny percentage on what you earn from renting it out."

He began to nod. "I think it's a great idea, Robin." Then slowly the old frown settled back in place. "But I don't know if the banker will regard it as a successful venture. I can hear him now," he said, lowering his voice, mimicking Spencer's monotone. "Craig, what experience have you had in running a guest ranch?"

Robin took a deep breath. "Let me talk to Uncle—"

"No!" His voice was low yet firm, the same tone he used with the boys to let them know he meant business. "That I will not do. Listen, Robin, I think you've come up with a great idea, and I'll always be grateful if it works out. And we can talk about the cabin and your investment in it. But the rest of it, the financing—I have to get that on my own. Otherwise, I won't do it."

The look in his eyes told her he meant it. She had learned about his pride, and she knew if he couldn't handle this himself, the plan would go no further than just talking about it.

"All right Craig, you handle it. I'll stay in the background. I just want to help," she added softly.

"You've helped me more than I can ever say. Last night—"

"Dad!" Zack bounded into the room. "Can the Walton guys come over today?"

"We'll see about it, Zack." He glanced across the table at Robin as though remembering something. "Tell you what. The boys can come over if you'll let Robin work with you on your spelling. You know you have a problem there."

"Can you spell horse, Zack?" Robin asked him.

"H-O-R-S-E," he rallied back.

"Great. We'll start with animals, move on to some other words, then end up with animals again. As long as you pay attention," she stressed. "Now first, what about breakfast?"

"I'm not hungry." Zack frowned.

"Look, why don't we keep it simple this morning?" Craig suggested. "What about cereal? I'm going down to have a word with Harley and Sam, then I'm coming back to do some work in my office. Robin, if you have a little time, say…," he glanced at the clock, "a couple of hours from now, maybe you could come in the office and help with some paperwork?"

"Sounds better than cooking bacon and eggs," she quipped, getting up to pour juice for Zack.

Twenty-Two

ater as Robin studied Craig's plans on paper, she could see some marvelous ideas taking shape. He had methodically outlined a route for trail rides and designated an area for chuck wagon suppers, tent camping, guest facilities, and finally some classes in horseback riding. He had sketched in additional facilities to board horses for people who wanted a horse but lived in town.

"Once I started working on this, I saw the possibilities are even better than we first thought. In addition to trail rides, we could have wildlife photo trips up into the mountains. There's plenty of game here."

"Wonderful."

"And we could have a morning roundup from Horsethief Park, the high meadow. Guests could get in on that, going with Harley and Sam and me to round up the horses for the day. It's actually a lot of fun," he grinned, staring into space.

"And everyone could meet back here for an authentic cowboy breakfast," Robin suggested.

He looked back at her, his dark eyes glowing with hope. "Hey, that's a good idea, too."

Glancing at the way he had outlined his plans on paper, she saw that he was being careful and analytical about each step.

"Looks like you're good at planning. Didn't know you were so organized," she said with a nudge.

"I'm finally putting those college courses to use. In one of them I did well when three of us worked together in setting up a dummy business. My instructor was a stickler for laying the groundwork." He pointed to his outline. "This is the groundwork."

She snapped her fingers, another brainstorm hitting her. "Craig, I have a friend whose father owns a travel agency in Calgary. He started out small, just booking accommodations for the Stampede, but he was good at what he did, and now he has agencies in Vancouver, Toronto, and Montreal. I could call Mr. Fisher and see what he thinks, so far as sending tourists here."

He nodded. "Sure. If you don't mind."

"Craig, this whole plan," her hand swept over the notepad, "is the answer. I just know it is." She could hardly contain her enthusiasm. "We just have to step forward in faith and believe that it can happen."

He pushed back from the desk, placing a hand around his neck to massage the tense muscles. "You must have been doing some big-time praying last night," he grinned sheepishly.

"I was! And I have a feeling you were too, Craig. It is totally out of character for my eyelids to pop open before eight o'clock without the help of a shrill alarm, which I tossed in the wastebasket after the school year ended."

"You what?" he laughed.

"Every morning for months I had been wanting to hurl that thing as far as I could. On the last day of school, I settled for hurling it into the wastebasket. This school year, I'll have to buy another one."

Craig looked at her, not daring to voice the thoughts in his head. He could hardly believe what he was thinking, but he liked the feel of it. He could imagine Robin right here with them, a part of their lives...

He dropped his eyes to the papers on his desk. Of course they couldn't go on living under the same roof, with her bedroom just down the hall from his. It wouldn't look right.

A small grin kicked at the corner of his mouth. But it would feel right. Slowly, he looked back to her face, staring into the hazel eyes that sparkled and danced beneath her thick red hair. She had been caught up in their project and was unaware she often plowed through her hair with her fingers, leaving a few strands out of place. But he liked that about her. She was spontaneous and open and comfortable with him and the boys.

"What in the world are you thinking?" she asked.

"Hmm?"

"You must be imagining yourself on a trail ride," she said smiling at him. "You looked so happy."

He looked at her and thought about how much he liked being with her, how she was changing his life from despair to joy.

"I am happy," he said.

"Then get busy rounding up your financing. I'm dying to start on those chuck wagon suppers before the summer gets further gone."

He nodded. "You know, we could do that now. I still have a little money stashed back. I was going to use it for a new roof on the house and some outside repairs. But maybe I won't have to sell the place, after all." He stood up and crossed around to her side, extending his hand to her.

She reached out and he pulled her gently from the chair to

173

his side. "Thanks." He dipped his head, savoring the taste of her lips, sweet as honey, and he could feel his heart hammering against his chest as he kissed her.

"Woops, hold it," she said, flattening her palms against his chest and pressing gently. "You're getting out of line, cowboy."

He chuckled, releasing her. "It's getting harder to stay in line, teacher. In fact, it might be a good idea to keep your distance from me."

"And just why is that?" she asked, her eyes issuing the dare of a game.

"Because I'm no longer thinking of you as a cook. Or a teacher." He bent down, nuzzling his cheek against her soft hair with its subtle, pleasant fragrance. As he breathed in her scent, he realized for the first time that at last it was safe to admit it. He was falling in love with Robin Grayson.

Twenty-Three

By the next morning, Robin and Craig were unable to keep their plans to themselves. Craig had asked Sam and Harley's opinion on the idea; he needed to be assured they would stay on at the ranch so that he could count on their help in this project. And Robin had called her friend in Calgary.

"I could send him as much business as he wants," Fisher said, upon hearing the theme of the ranch would be keeping the frontier spirit alive. "I have clients as far away as Germany and Japan who are begging for this sort of place. If the ranch is run well, I can almost guarantee its success."

He had even offered to write a letter, sending copies of tourist requests to assist Craig in getting a loan.

Both Craig and Robin were enthusiastic about the way things were taking shape. In fact, Harley had been pestering him since daybreak with an idea.

At the end of the day, Craig and Robin sat in his office, going over the plans again, when Harley's head popped around the door.

"I knew I had seen a chuck wagon somewhere, one I think

could be bought." Harley was breathless with excitement.

Craig looked up from a column of figures he had been calling off to Robin as she added them on the calculator.

"Harley, could it wait until tomorrow?" Craig asked, mildly irritated by yet another interruption.

"I'm afraid it can't." He was wearing his brown Levi's, a blue plaid western shirt, and a special belt buckle he had won rodeoing years before. His hair was awry, his hat was missing, and he looked as though he had run all the way to the house. He kept fidgeting with the door as though he couldn't contain his excitement one more second.

"Okay," Craig glanced at Robin, a brow lifted, "tell us what you have in mind, Harley."

"Well," Harley took a deep breath, making a conscious effort to speak slowly, clearly. "It's about that chuck wagon. I know where to get it, and I can buy it for a song."

Robin and Craig both leaned forward, their attention captured by his promise.

"Great. Where is it, Harley?"

"It's down toward Bonners Ferry." A flicker of doubt crossed his face, but he quickly recovered. "Actually, it may be over in that valley out from Crestin. But I know this." He leaned back on his wiry legs, looking smug. "If I can find Rod Hunter—"

"Who's Rod Hunter?"

"Oh, he's a cowboy friend, a guy who used to be on the rodeo circuit with me. Anyway, Rod was with me when we saw it. We'd been down to the border—" He cut that off quickly and made another start. "It was sitting under the shed of a barn near a ranch house. I remember we were jawing with the woman, a widow lady she was…" His eyes drifted into space for a moment.

Craig and Robin exchanged speculative glances.

"Anyway, Rod's ranching out from Cranbrook now. I can pick up Rod and we'll head down there and come back with that chuck wagon. That's a promise, Craig. Uh, I'd need to borrow your truck. Mine ain't got the horsepower or even a decent trailer hitch to it."

"I don't know, Harley." Craig could imagine Harley and Rod getting sidetracked down at the border at the Good Grief Saloon for a couple of days.

"This is strictly business, Mr. Cameron." Harley's expression was grim as he looked Craig squarely in the eye. "You have my word on it. I can even call you on your shortwave radio at Eastport."

Robin reached over, squeezing Craig's hand. He didn't have to look at her to know she was encouraging him to trust Harley.

"Harley, do you think that chuck wagon is still there? Sounds as though it's been a while."

He nodded solemnly. "She said she'd never part with it. Had some wonderful memories attached to it."

"Then why would she part with it now?"

"Well," Harley scratched his chin, "I'm not just positive she would. But I believe if she thought it was going for a good cause—something that would make other folks' lives a little better…" He hesitated, nodding slowly. "She just struck me as the kind of woman who'd do things for other people."

"Of course we'll pay her whatever she feels is fair."

"I'll get Rod to help me. And we can round up another cowboy or two to load the thing and haul it back on Rod's trailer."

Craig took a deep breath, wavering for a moment. Did he dare trust Harley with his truck? "Okay," he finally replied.

Harley blinked, obviously surprised that Craig was agreeing to the plan. Then he jerked his small frame upright and thrust his chest out. "I'll leave first thing in the morning."

"Do you want Sam to go along with you?" Craig called after Harley, as he made for the door.

"No, sir," he called back. "Sam's got plenty to do here."

The back door slammed, and Craig looked across at Robin.

"I know what you're thinking," she said, "but we have to give him a chance. He just may locate that chuck wagon and bring it back. Otherwise, where will we come up with one?"

Craig shrugged. "It might be cheaper to build the thing from scratch rather than send Harley off with my truck and some of his rodeo buddies."

Her hand rested lightly on his palm, and now she laced her fingers through his, trying to emphasize her words. "Think of the character that old chuck wagon will have."

Craig laughed. "Think of the rust and repairs."

"But you won't be moving it again, will you?"

"No." He looked at the plan before him. "I'm going to put the picnic site up at Middle Meadow."

"So, a chuck wagon with character is exactly what you need."

He reached for her, pulling her against his chest.

"You make everything seem better. And you're right. I do need to trust Harley." He frowned. "I don't know why I find it hard to trust people. Maybe it's just in my genes. Dad's a great guy, but he has a tendency to wonder if someone has an angle when they do something nice for him."

Robin nodded. "I know. Maybe that's part of human nature. But I think you can count on Harley this time."

Craig shook his head, still fighting doubts. "I hope so."

Twenty-Four

❦

The next morning when Harley cranked up the truck, Craig took a deep breath and told Robin he would try to forget how many payments were left on it. They were having their morning coffee, studying the legal pad that was quickly filling up with details.

"Dad!" Will burst into the room, breathless. "Harley's taking your pickup off somewhere and—"

"I know, Will." He smiled kindly at his son, who always seemed so concerned about everything. "I gave him permission."

Will looked from Craig to Robin, clearly puzzled.

"Maybe it's time you looked over our plan for chuck wagon suppers, Will. Give us an opinion." Craig smiled at his son.

Robin had released Craig's hand when Will burst into the room, but now her affection was all for Will. She reached out an arm. "Here, come sit me with me. You can see better."

Shyly, Will walked over and settled himself into her chair, sharing a corner with her. He held his back rigid, and he kept his body distanced from her. Her heart constricted. Poor Will, so afraid to love again.

Casually, she put an arm around his shoulder and looked down at him. "Will, we want to know what you think about this."

Slowly, she felt his rigid shoulders begin to relax against her. She rested her chin on his head, breathing the fresh sunshine in his soft brown hair and feeling her heart melt with love for this dear little boy.

Harley had driven off early Thursday morning, and by Saturday morning Craig was pacing the front porch, staring down the deserted road.

"I never should have let him talk me into that," he argued to Will, who sat quietly on the porch, also staring at the road.

"He'll be back, Dad."

Zack and Robin were on the sofa in the living room, going over spelling words from Zack's school papers. She could see that Zack would be a good speller if he just focused.

"Look, Zack, you've missed some easy ones," she pointed out.

He shrugged, fidgeting on the sofa, glancing toward the front door.

"I'll bet these words are too easy for you. Let me give you a hard one. Spell Kootenay."

His blond head swiveled around. "I can't spell that!"

She laughed. "In Canada it's spelled K-O-O-T-E-N-A-Y. Then, once the river crosses the border into Montana and Idaho, the word is spelled K-O-O-T-E-N-A-I."

He peered into her face. "Are you nervous?"

She laughed. "I guess I am. Do I sound like it?"

He nodded. "Your voice sounds kinda pinched." He looked at his spelling papers. "We don't have big words like that yet."

"I know. I'm just being silly trying to take our minds off our worries." Might as well be honest, she decided. Who wasn't nervous? They were all practically biting their nails. "Tell you what, why don't we just put your work away until Monday? I think we're all too nervous to concentrate."

"What if Harley doesn't come back?" Zack asked, looking at her wide-eyed.

Robin took a deep breath. "We just have to keep our faith up."

He tilted his head, staring up at her curiously. "Our faith in Harley or our faith in God?"

She smiled and affectionately tousled his blond hair. "In both, Zack." Her eyes lifted over his head to the porch. And silently she began to breathe a desperate prayer. *Oh Lord, please don't let Harley disappoint us.*

Robin decided to plan a picnic lunch for them, since they were all jumpy and nervous and needed a distraction.

Craig had grown very quiet, Will was looking at her with doubt written all over his face, and Zack was practically bouncing off the wall. Craig had planned for the three of them to go down and help Sam construct a frame for the expansion of the barn. But it was obvious that nobody could concentrate enough for that. Even Sam had wandered up, settled his lanky frame into a rocker, and begun to pelt Craig with questions.

Through the open door, Robin could hear a few words at random: "More wood...better tools..."

Then Craig's voice rose above Sam's quiet monotone.

"Sam, give it a rest. Until Harley gets back with my truck, I'm putting everything on hold. Go on into town if you want. After all, this is the weekend. You deserve a break."

Robin could hear the rocker lurch, and she thought Sam must have bolted from his chair in his eagerness to head for town. He made a brief stop at the back door and poked his head in.

"Robin, are you gonna have that singing again in the morning?"

Robin stared at him for a moment. She couldn't believe it was almost Sunday again. "Yes, I am, Sam. As long as I'm here, we'll be having some sort of worship service on Sunday mornings. Why don't you bring Lucille and Kelsey back tomorrow?"

A wide grin shot across his face. "I'll do that if nobody minds. They had a real good time last week."

"I'm glad."

"Lucille already asked if she could bring something to help with the lunch."

Robin's first impulse was to decline, and then she decided it would make Lucille feel more welcome if she contributed to their get-together.

"What does she like to cook, Sam?"

Sam's grin widened even further, tickling the lobes of his ears. "She makes real good potato salad."

"Perfect! Will you ask her if she'd mind bringing some potato salad? That'll go well with the hamburgers."

"Yes'm. Kelsey likes hamburgers."

"Good. And Sam, I think you guys are doing a good job with Kelsey. It'll just take a little time, and she'll be fine."

His eyes were sad for a moment as a worried frown crossed his face. "You're probably right. The thing is, 'til that gal gets her head on straight, me and Lucille got a little problem standing in our way."

"I know. But you two look happy together. I think it'll work out."

The sadness left his eyes, and he stepped back in the kitchen. Glancing toward the porch, he lowered his voice. "I ain't the only one looking happy around here. Keep up the good work." He grinned at her, then ducked his head as though he had already said too much. Stretching his long legs, he bounded out the door, whistling a hymn as he disappeared toward the bunkhouse.

Robin thought about what he had said as she laid out lettuce leaves for tuna sandwiches. Just when she thought she was making progress with Craig and the boys, something happened to set her back. If Harley let them all down, she would feel partly responsible. After all, she had pressed Craig to trust Harley. She recalled what he had told her about his dad's reluctance to trust and made a mental note never to make a promise to Craig unless she could keep it.

Craig entered the kitchen, holding a sack in his hands. Robin couldn't help noticing the sack held the emblem of a western wear store in Fort Steele.

"Since we're going horseback riding this afternoon, I have something for you." He extended the sack to Robin.

"Why, thanks." She opened the sack and pulled out a soft, white felt cowboy hat. "Craig, how sweet!" She was about to give him a big hug when Zack and Will stepped into the room, each sporting a new hat.

"I got the boys hats, too."

"They look great," she said, glancing from Will's tan suede hat to Zack's darker one.

She told herself that he was buying everyone hats, not just one for her, so that made hers less special. She pushed the thought away, however, as she placed her hat on her head, tilting it at an angle over her red hair.

"What do you guys think?"

Zack merely laughed at her, but Will studied the hat and replied solemnly. "It looks nice on you."

"Thanks, Will." She smiled down at him, genuinely pleased by those words. It was the first time he had complimented her. She glanced at Craig and caught a quick wink.

She turned back to the boys. "Well, I'll have our lunch made in fifteen minutes flat. Will those horses be ready?"

The guys bolted for the door and raced toward the barn. Craig lingered in the kitchen, leaning forward to remove her hat from her head and give her a kiss that took her breath away.

"You're the prettiest cowboy I've ever kissed," he said, trailing his lips across her cheek and up to her forehead, where he planted another kiss.

"I should hope so," she teased, trying to recapture her wits. "I certainly wouldn't want you to go around kissing any old cowboy."

He was about to kiss her again when Will and Zack's voices drifted to them. Another argument was obviously in progress, and Craig merely shook his head and turned for the back door.

They had planned to ride up to Middle Meadow for their picnic, but on an impulse, Robin had suggested going on to the cabin. The boys were up for it, and even Craig smiled agreeably.

"Okay." He glanced up at the sunny sky. "Don't think we have any rain in the forecast."

"Dad, it never rains," Will scolded, but he, too, was smiling.

"And if I told Sam to knock off work on Saturday," Craig continued, "its the least I can do for the rest of us. In fact," he looked at Robin, "maybe we should be going into town to do something fun."

"Dad, this is fun," Zack shouted.

He was perched on top of Jake, a slow, surefooted sorrel. Will rode a dark bay that he had named King, and Robin had chosen Sugar again. Craig rode Chief.

"Look at those crows." Will pointed to the large black birds circling the sky.

"They're ravens," Craig answered. "They look like crows, only they're two or three times as big."

"I know the difference in ravens and crows." Zack twisted in his saddle, shooting a superior look at Will. "And I know about camp robbers, too, don't I, Dad?"

Craig and Robin exchanged amused glances.

"What are camp robbers, Zack?"

"They're those birds that come sneaking around when we're having a picnic."

"Everybody knows that, Zack," Will fussed.

"Okay, you two, we're going to have fun today, and that means no arguments."

"Dad, I bet I know your favorite kind of bird," Zack said, his blue eyes dancing.

"A blue jay," Will spoke up. "Only the ones in the States are prettier than here."

"These have more gray to them," Craig agreed. "But no, it isn't my favorite bird. What do you think it is, Zack?"

"A robin! Like that one." Zack pointed to Robin, proud of his joke. Craig and Robin laughed, and even Will joined in, appreciating Zack's little pun.

Robin looked at the boys. "I was named for the robins, you know. My parents couldn't wait for spring each year so they could take us camping and fishing. They always said when robins came into our yard they were either bringing spring or telling us it was on the way. And since I was born in April, I guess they thought Robin was the perfect name for me."

"And you have red-orange hair, like a robin's breast," Zack spoke up.

Once they reached the cabin site, they turned their horses into the grassy meadow, and the boys jumped down and began to explore the yard.

"Hey guys," Robin called to them, "Come look at my great-grandfather's name carved over the door."

They rushed up, staring with open mouths, obviously fascinated.

"Tell you what," Craig said, "why don't I carve our initials over there in that tree? After all, this place has significance for us as well."

As her eyes met his, she saw something warm and caring there, and she knew the significance definitely included her. She smiled, wondering if it was really possible to be this happy or whether she should start worrying that it was too good to be true.

Don't be ridiculous, she told herself as they found the perfect tree and Craig pulled out his Case knife.

"Whose initials are you gonna put first?" Zack wanted to know.

Robin put an arm around his shoulder. "I think it should be yours and Will's, and then your dad's."

"And yours," Will added, looking up at her.

She smiled at him, hoping that at last she was winning him over.

Craig took his time, carving each letter perfectly. When he was done, they all stood back and admired his work.

"I'm starved," Zack said, looking around for the picnic sack.

They had lunch under the same tree where Robin and Craig had sat talking. And where Craig had first kissed her. Their eyes met over the thermos of juice, and another special look passed between them. When she dragged her eyes from Craig, she saw Will watching them, and she reminded herself to tread carefully. She didn't want to do anything to jeopardize the delicate relationship that she was forming with the boys.

"Here comes the camp robbers." Zack pointed to the gray bird sailing down near them, watching them curiously. Another one joined him, and Robin tossed a crust of bread to them.

The first bird jumped on the bread as the other one edged nearer to Robin. She took another crust and extended it; the bird inched its way toward her while everyone watched in fascination. Slowly, the bird came closer and closer while nobody moved.

Robin kept her arm still, stretched out to the bird, and finally he came right up, grabbed the piece of bread, and flew off. Everyone laughed, watching him sail back to a distance to enjoy his treat.

"I've never been able to get them to come to me," Craig said, as they watched the other bird inch closer to Will's outstretched hand.

"Maybe I'm more gentle than you," Robin teased.

"You are." Craig smiled at her, and again Robin felt a sense of satisfaction just getting him to smile. And he was smiling often.

Later, after a fun-filled afternoon, they rode back to the house, weary yet happy.

Once they crested the hill and had a view of the ranch, Will pointed and yelled.

"Dad! Here comes Harley pulling a stage coach!"

All heads turned toward the road, and indeed Harley was driving Craig's truck, pulling a flatbed trailer with...the chuck wagon!

"He got it!" Robin yelled.

All horses were put into a gallop as they raced home to hear Harley's story.

Twenty-Five

❧

O nce they had unloaded the chuck wagon, everyone circled it, touched it, admired it, and complimented Harley again and again. The chuck wagon was in remarkably good shape with a sturdy frame and wheels intact.

"Yep, I made a deal with Ms. Brown for the chuck wagon." Harley's chest swelled with importance. "She's one of the nicest ladies I ever met. Promised her a special weekend here, and Craig—you'd better send pictures of Will and Zack. I explained about their momma…"

Robin winced and tried not to look at Craig and the boys to see how they were taking the news that Harley had used them to play on her sympathy.

"How much did she accept?"

"Gave her the two hundred you sent along. And I added another hundred for good measure. She was satisfied." He turned to Zack and Will. "Now, boys, I know you never seen one of these, so I'll just explain it to you. Come here to the back of the thing, first." At the rear of one side, facing aft, he lowered a hinged lid and revealed a short cookstove in its own compartment.

"See, this lid is on a swinging leg. I can stand the leg up, and now we have a table. And the little stove fits right in there."

"That's a stove to cook on?" Will was fascinated.

"Yep. A genuine wood-burning stove. See here, it's got these six pieces of stovepipe that fit together to make a chimney."

Will turned to Robin. "He makes 'chimney' sound like 'chimley.'"

"Around here on the side," Harley forged on, "we keep silverware and cooking gadgets in these drawers."

"Looks like a Victorian desk," Robin said, staring at all the drawers and cubbyholes. She opened a tiny drawer and peered in, finding a rusty can opener.

"Can I ride in the chuck wagon with you, Harley?" Zack wanted to know.

"Son, we're not going to be driving it," Craig explained. "We're going to take it up to Middle Meadow and park it, and that's where we'll have our chuck wagon suppers. Sam is going to build some picnic tables and benches, and we'll put in a barbecue pit."

"Look, Craig." Harley removed a piece of canvas tarp. "We can cover it with this when it's not in use."

The excitement was contagious.

"Dad, can we have a chuck wagon supper tonight?"

Craig hesitated. "Well, we don't have the thing cleaned up yet, Will. We'll have to do some work..."

"Would you settle for a cookout out here in the yard beside the chuck wagon?" Robin asked, grinning at Will.

"Great idea," Craig said.

Later, they sat around the campfire, roasting the first dozen wieners, laughing at one of Harley's stories. It was not yet dark, but twilight was quickly settling over them.

Robin munched on her sandwich and absorbed the tranquility of a summer evening at Sundance. "I guess you guys are accustomed to the peace and quiet here," she said, "but I really enjoy not hearing any cars racing up and down the road with their horns blowing."

"Or sirens," Harley frowned. "I just about wrecked—well, not really, Craig—but while I was in Cranbrook, I heard the siren of a police car, and it scared the wits out of me."

"I can see why," Craig grinned wryly.

Zack blurted something, spitting crumbs in his eagerness to speak.

"Wait until you finish chewing," Craig said.

Zack took a giant swallow and pointed up to the sky. "Sometimes we hear and see jet airplanes. Dad says they're probably going from Calgary or Edmonton all the way to California, maybe even Disneyland. When we see them, we know where they're going," he boasted, glancing from Robin back to the sky. "Will, I bet those people can look down and see our horses out in the meadow."

"Zack, they can't see our horses," Will argued. "If they did, they wouldn't look as big as rats!"

Harley chuckled and reached for his pipe as though he was preparing to spin another tall tale, when the rumble of thunder reached them.

"I've been watching that cloud back there," Craig said, pointing to the west.

"Dadblast it, it's gonna rain!" Harley said, leaping to his feet to glare at the sky.

"Does that mean we can't camp out like you promised, Dad?"

"Harley and I can sleep under the chuck wagon," Zack said, his eyes pulling at Harley for support.

"Zack, these old bones are a little tired for the hard ground."

"But——"

"Zack, there'll be plenty of other nights we can camp out. We've got a storm brewing tonight." Craig pointed to the cloud where slivers of lightning began to dance.

Robin jumped up, collecting food and dishes.

The boys were starting to complain until Craig put up a hand, silencing them. "Hey, guys, we need the rain, so let's try to be good sports. Finish your hot dogs, then we'd better head inside. Harley, let's wrap that canvas over the chuck wagon."

Harley was stomping around the back of the wagon, fussing to himself. He was having as much fun as Zack and Will and was every bit as disappointed over the rain as they were.

"There'll be other nights to camp out," Robin reminded them. "And besides, I'm in the mood for a hot game of Monopoly."

Will was standing beside her, stacking the silverware into a pan. "You're just saying that to be nice," he said quietly.

"You're right, I am. But, we might as well make the most of a rainy night, don't you think?"

Will nodded. "And we have plenty of hotels."

Twenty-Six

S am, Lucille, and Kelsey arrived just before ten on Sunday morning. Harley, Craig, and the boys were lounging around the porch, listening to Robin strum the guitar. It was a beautiful Sunday morning, the birds were singing, and everyone was in a great mood.

Zack and Will had showered and looked nice in clean jeans and T-shirts, their faces scrubbed, their hair glistening from a shampoo. Robin had put on her best shirt and Levi's, and she had even polished her boots.

As Lucille and Kelsey got out of Sam's truck and headed up to the porch, Robin picked up the tempo on the guitar.

"What kind of music is that?" Kelsey said in greeting.

"It's a spiritual I learned from one of my students in Charleston. She said it was her grandmother's favorite and that she used to sing it on Sundays in New Orleans."

"Wait'll you guys taste Lucille's potato salad," Sam bragged, as Lucille waved to the group, then hurried inside to put the dish in the refrigerator.

"Since it's Sunday, is anyone going to say a prayer?" Will asked after they finished a hymn.

Craig cleared his throat. "I'll say one."

Robin turned startled eyes to him, then lowered her head. It was a short prayer, giving thanks for family and friends, good music, and good food.

Afterward everyone rushed to the dining room where the food was set up in huge containers, buffet style, with tall glasses of iced tea.

Kelsey wore a more conservative T-shirt, and her hair was plaited in a single braid which Robin complimented.

"Thanks," Kelsey said, looking around the living room. Zack was walking by her side, and Robin thought it interesting that he was gravitating toward Kelsey.

"You guys don't even have a television?" Kelsey gasped, as though she couldn't believe her eyes.

"We don't want one," Zack boasted.

Craig was standing at the table, passing out plates. Overhearing the conversation, he looked at Kelsey.

"We're surrounded by high mountains and can't get the reception we need for television."

"Not anywhere in this valley?" Kelsey asked, horrified.

"Dad says there's nothing good on TV anymore," Zack said, watching Kelsey's reaction. "There's more bad than good."

"Not for me," Kelsey responded.

"She can't make it without MTV," Lucille laughed, while sending a flirting glance in Sam's direction.

Robin had noticed that their eyes had locked more than once during the morning, and it seemed they were more open with their affection.

"Well," Kelsey said, taking a plate and peering at all the food on the table, "I'd be bored to death without television."

"Heaven forbid that you be bored," Lucille whooped.

Kelsey gave her mother a sharp glance, obviously not finding the remark humorous.

"I started to plan a picnic around the chuck wagon," Robin intervened, "but our wiener roast got rained out last night, so I wasn't sure about today."

"This is perfect," Craig said, smiling at Robin.

"Mr. Cameron, are we going horseback riding today?" Kelsey turned her attention back to Craig.

"Sure, if everyone wants to."

"I want to," Zack yelled from the opposite end of the table.

Soon everyone had their plates loaded with hamburgers, potato salad, and all the trimmings, and the talking quieted down.

As they were cleaning up, Lucille snagged Robin's arm. "I want to talk to you later, if you have time."

Robin looked at her. She was wearing a denim vest with lots of bangles and beads on it over a bright pink T-shirt and pink Levi's. Robin hesitated. She had planned to go horseback riding, but she could see from the look in Lucille's eyes that something was up. "Sure, how about when we're done here?"

Later, after the dishes were done and everyone shooed off to the barn, Lucille and Robin sat down in the porch rockers. Then Lucille turned anxiously to Robin.

"Robin, I wanted to ask you a favor."

"What is it?" Robin mentally tried to leap ahead, certain the "favor" must concern Sam.

"Well," Lucille took a deep breath, glancing toward the barn. Obviously what she had to say was confidential.

"Don't worry. They're halfway to the back forty by now," Robin assured her.

"It's about Kelsey. She's been going out with a boy who's a lot older than she is. He's already out of school, singing in a rock band, and..." Her voice trailed as she shook her head. "I just don't feel good about it, but if I try to say anything, she just looks at me with that smirk…like, well, she wouldn't respect anything I have to say."

"Why not? You're her mother."

"I know, but…"

"You know, Lucille, my mom always told me that she made mistakes like everyone else on this earth. But she was still my mother, and she expected me to mind her. And I did."

Lucille looked thoughtful. "I've just hated to say anything."

"Well, don't. You have to be honest with her. In my opinion, one of the most important things in any relationship is honesty. Kids today really pick up on that. I know I kind of expected Mom or Dad to rope me back in line when I was about to get out of the fence. Maybe I didn't want them to, but I was always relieved when they did. Seemed strange, but that was how I felt."

Lucille smiled at her. "You're such a good person. I bet they never had any problems with you."

"Oh, I was pretty headstrong. And you know the old saying about redheads having a temper. Well, in my case, it's true."

They both laughed at that, and then Lucille grew serious again.

"Since we're talking personally, how do you think Sam feels about me?"

"Do you mean…?"

Lucille shifted nervously in her chair. "I mean, well, Sam has never been married, you know, and I just wonder if he's sure about me. He says he loves me, but…"

"Then I think you can believe him. Sam seems to be a very honest guy. I don't believe he would lie to you."

Tears of joy filled Lucille's eyes as she looked over at Robin. "Thanks!" She turned and looked toward the barn. "I can tell Mr. Cameron loves you."

That took Robin by surprise. "Why do you say that? I mean, how can you tell?"

"By the way he looks at you."

"Oh?" Robin thought back to those glowing dark eyes, wondering. "Well, he's never told me so." As soon as she spoke those words, she clamped her lips shut. What was she doing sitting here talking so personally with Lucille, who was sure to tell Sam, who was sure to tell Harley? Then they might as well get a megaphone and broadcast it over Caribou Creek.

"He probably won't tell you; at least, not for a while." Lucille sighed. "When he first came here with those little boys, Sam said he was the saddest fellow he'd ever seen. Just sat and stared all the time, or else he was grumpy. Except to the boys. He's always been a wonderful father. Everyone knows that."

Robin nodded, looking over at Lucille. "Yes, he is." She wanted to put an end to this conversation. She couldn't explain why, but she felt that she was betraying Craig to sit and talk about him with Lucille. "Look, why don't we walk down to the corral and wait for them? I see the first rider coming over the hill now."

Lucille hesitated, obviously wanting to continue their chat, but then she turned her head and caught sight of Sam and leaped to her feet.

"Listen, in case we don't get a chance to talk again, I want you to know how much I appreciate what you've done for Kelsey."

Robin shrugged and stood. "I don't feel that I've done anything." They walked down the porch steps and turned toward the corral.

"Oh, but you have. She's been easier to live with, and I think it has a lot to do with the time we're spending out here. Of course she wouldn't in a million years admit that she's having a good time or that she looks forward to it. But I know she does."

"Good. I'm glad. And she really is a great gal."

Lucille studied Robin suspiciously for a few seconds, then began to grin. "Yeah, I guess so."

Later, the group sat around a new picnic table Sam had built, sipping iced drinks while Harley told stories.

When the laughter died down, Sam looked across at Lucille. "The day's wearing on, so I'll head down to the barn and groom the horses and see what else needs doing before we go."

"Maybe Harley and I will pitch in." Craig stood and stretched.

Robin looked at the boys. "Who wants to go hiking?"

"I do!" Zack yelled.

"I'll go," Will agreed.

Robin looked at Kelsey. "What about you?"

She was still working at not being spontaneous. "I don't know. Where would we go?"

"We could go up to that first meadow and look for arrowheads," Will said, looking hopefully at Robin.

"Oh, that sounds like a great idea," Robin agreed.

"I don't know," Kelsey said, although Robin could see by the look in her eyes that she was up for it.

"Think I'll go too," Lucille said. "I need to walk off a few pounds."

"You can't do it in one afternoon, Mom," Kelsey quipped. But as she looked at her mother, her expression was no longer angry or accusing, and she spoke in a teasing tone of voice.

"Sounds like a great idea," Craig smiled at Robin. "We'll be through in about an hour."

"We'd better get our backpack," Will said to Zack, and they both tore out for the house.

"Their backpack?" Kelsey echoed, staring after them. "I thought we were only going for a hike."

Robin smiled. "We are. They just want to make the most of it."

"Yeah," Lucille was all smiles. "You know how boys are."

"No, because I don't have a little brother."

Robin cleared her throat. "Let's head on. The boys will catch up with us."

"They'll probably pass us in no time," Lucille laughed as they walked across the yard.

The sun was beaming down, but the breeze that drifted up from Clear Creek felt good. Robin was pleased with the way the day was going so far.

"Robin, I have a new boyfriend," Kelsey said, glancing at her mother.

The smile vanished from Lucille's face.

"You'd probably like him, Robin."

"Oh?" Robin peered across at her. "Why is that?"

"He plays the guitar, too."

"What kind of music?"

"Hard rock. He travels with a band and has a really neat life. They go everywhere."

"You know, Robin, I was thinking about something this morning when we were singing," Lucille broke in. Her change of subject was painfully obvious. "We could all go to church in Skookumchuck some time. I was raised in a little church there. It's nondenominational, and everyone is friendly. Or they used to be," she added, frowning down at the pebbles beneath her feet.

"Sure, we'll plan to go sometime. Then maybe you and Kelsey and I could go shopping down in Cranbrook. I need to do some shopping."

Kelsey looked at her. "What kind of shopping?"

"Clothes, of course. I didn't bring a lot of clothes with me, and I've lived in jeans and T-shirts for too long. I think it's time I bought a skirt and blouse."

"I know a place that has neat stuff," Kelsey volunteered.

Footsteps thudded up the path behind them, and Robin glanced over her shoulder.

"Wait for us," Zack yelled. He and Will were flying over the path, both wearing their cowboy hats, their backpacks strapped on. As they approached, Robin saw that Will had a small leather pouch attached to his belt. She knew he was hoping to find some arrowheads, and she reminded herself to look twice as hard so he wouldn't be disappointed.

She glanced toward the woods bordering the meadow. "You know, if we're going to help Will find some arrowheads, we might need to hike around the edge of those woods over there."

Everyone agreed and headed in that direction. Soon, they came to a fork in the trail and Robin looked from Zack to Will. "Which way do you guys think we should go?

One fork led to the right; the other veered left back toward the creek.

"To the left," Zack said.

"No, to the right," Will pointed. "It leads deeper into the woods, but then it winds back toward the main road."

Everyone had stopped, looking right and left.

"Decisions, decisions," Lucille laughed. "That's life, isn't it? Always having to make decisions."

"Dad says trails are like life," Will said solemnly, looking at Lucille. "That we have to be careful which trail we take, or we may end up in the wrong place."

"Your dad's right," Lucille said, looking emotional. "I've taken a few wrong trails myself." Her eyes strayed to Kelsey, who suddenly appeared uncomfortable with the subject.

"I think we should take the right fork," Will said.

"Okay, we'll try the right fork this time," Robin agreed. "And next time, Zack, we'll try the left fork, your way."

"Are you gonna put up a sign and name the forks?" Zack looked at her wide-eyed.

"You mean like Zack's Fork and Will's Fork?" Robin asked

"Maybe," he nodded, pleased with the idea. "We could do that."

"Not today," Kelsey complained.

"Right." Robin turned to Will. "Lead the way down your trail."

"Short cuts," Lucille spoke up suddenly. "In my life I've learned something about short cuts. The quick, easy way isn't always the right way. Or the one that looks the most exciting may lead to a dead end."

"You sure are getting philosophical, Mom," Kelsey drawled. "Any special reason?"

Lucille shrugged, avoiding Kelsey's eyes.

"How do you decide, Robin?" Kelsey asked. The smirk she had worn last Sunday had dissolved into a grin now. And while Robin knew that Kelsey was baiting her, she decided to make the most of her answer.

"If we're talking about life's decisions, I try to go by what feels good in my soul."

"If it feels good, do it," Kelsey quipped, turning her eyes to her mother to test her reaction.

"I said if it feels good in my soul," Robin reminded her. "There can be a difference."

"Yeah," Zack joined in. "Like chocolate cake feels good in my mouth, but too much hurts my belly."

They all laughed at Zack's analogy and trudged on. This time, Robin noticed, Kelsey had joined in the laughter good-naturedly Maybe she was coming around after all.

Twenty-Seven

After they had hiked a quarter mile, Lucille lagged back, taking a seat on a smooth log. "You guys go on. This old gal needs to rest. I'll wait here for you."

"Party pooper," Kelsey teased as they left her behind.

A hundred yards farther, Will and Zack stopped to examine a bird's nest on the ground, and Robin dropped down under the tree. "Hey, Kelsey, let's take a break."

The boys strayed a bit farther, but Robin could still keep them in sight. "So tell me about your boyfriend." She looked at Kelsey.

Kelsey shrugged. "I don't know. He's just a guy."

Robin arched a brow. "Not so special after all, huh?"

"The problem is..." She lowered her voice, finding the boys with her eyes as though being sure they were out of earshot. "He's been around, you know? He's been pushing me to do some things that..."

"That you know aren't right?"

"I didn't say they weren't right. Maybe not right for you," she said sarcastically.

Robin's eyes swept the girl's features, and she knew she was young and vulnerable and on the brink of making some big mistakes. "Well, you have to make your own choices. I remember when I was just about your age, something happened to change my thinking." She hesitated, determined not to push unless Kelsey was open to a conversation.

"What was it?" Kelsey asked softly.

"I had been seeing a guy in school who I didn't really like, but my parents objected to him, so that made him seem a little more glamorous, you know? What's that bit about forbidden fruit seeming sweeter?"

Kelsey laughed. "Yeah, I know what you mean."

"Then I let the youth director at our church talk me into going on a picnic up at Bow River with some other kids. His wife prepared fried chicken and made lots of goodies, and everyone liked the couple. They were great to us." She picked up a twig and began to break it in half, as she thought back to that summer.

"I remember Todd—that was the youth director—saying something on that trip that I've never forgotten. It was a beautiful day, and the guys were trying to throw rocks across the river. Todd pointed out what a wide river it was, but that it began as a little stream no wider than this." She held her hands six inches apart. "I couldn't imagine it. He said it was because the river began where the glaciers melted and ran together, picking up more streams along the way. He said our mistakes are like that. We can start with a little white lie, that builds into something bigger and bigger, until the first thing we know we're knee-deep in trouble. Pretty soon, we're in over our heads."

"Oh, I get your drift," Kelsey said, rocking back on her heels to give Robin a cynical look. "You're just saying that for my benefit, right?"

Robin shrugged lightly, trying not to take offense. "Nope, it's the truth. Why would I say something for your benefit when I don't know anything about your life or what you do? That doesn't make sense, does it?"

Kelsey frowned at the idea of doing something stupid. "So, what did you do about the boyfriend?"

Robin smiled. "I broke up with him."

Kelsey tilted her head back, regarding Robin thoughtfully.

"You're a very pretty girl, Kelsey," Robin spoke softly. "Take your time and make the right choices."

"Or I might end up like Mom!" she said bitterly.

"I don't see anything wrong with your mom. She's a warm, caring person who has a pleasant personality and tries to be nice to other people. And I like her potato salad," she added on a humorous note.

"I told you what she did—"

"And I told you I didn't want to hear it. She's still your mother, Kelsey, and you owe her some respect."

Just then the boys came bounding back, and Robin breathed a sigh of relief. The discussion needed to be ended before she said too much or Kelsey took offense.

"We can't find any arrowheads," Will said, looking hot and out of sorts.

"Well, you know what?" Robin said. "I think we need to plan another trip up to Skook's cabin, maybe camp overnight. That way we'd have plenty of time to look. And I'll bet we could find some up there."

"Yeah." Will's eyes lit up as he turned to Zack. "I'll race you back to the fork."

"You guys be careful," Robin called after them, then turned to Kelsey. "Ready to head back?"

"Yeah, Mom's probably wondering what happened to us."

Robin smiled at Kelsey and laid a hand lightly around her shoulder. "Know something? I like you, Kelsey."

They laughed together and started back down the trail.

Later, as the day came to an end and Sam drove off with Lucille and Kelsey, Craig dropped into the rocker and heaved a sigh. "I've worked up a king-sized headache today."

"Maybe you need some aspirin," Robin suggested.

The boys dragged off to bed without having to be told, and even Robin was exhausted.

"I'm going to hit the sack," she said.

"Sorry I'm bad company." Craig looked at her with a tentative smile that quickly faded.

"You're not bad company." She walked over to him and extended her hand. "I had fun today."

"I always have fun with you. You're great, know that?"

She shrugged. "Well, I always like to hear it."

Pulling her hand gently, he coaxed her onto his lap and looked up into her eyes. "I don't know what we did to deserve you in our lives, but I hope we don't mess up."

He pulled her closer, kissing her lips and sending her head into a spin. After a few minutes she broke away, looking down into his face and feeling breathless.

"You have a headache, remember? I don't want to make the patient worse."

"But—"

She silenced his protest by laying a finger over his lips, which he gently kissed, then she stood again. "Get a good night's rest," she said and forced herself to go back in the house and head to her room.

Twenty-Eight

C raig had left the house early for another appointment at the bank in Cranbrook.

"We'll plan a barbecue for the weekend if I get the loan." He grinned at her. "And we'll even invite your relatives."

"Then I'll start on the menu. You'll get the loan, Craig. All that paperwork you've done will sell itself."

Robin tried to remain positive until Craig drove off, but then she was suddenly attacked by a case of nerves.

She paced the kitchen restlessly. She opened the back door, feeling the summer morning breeze sweep over her, cooling her flushed cheeks. She wandered around the back yard to peer down at the bunkhouse. Sam, Harley, and the boys were out around the corral, fooling with the horses.

As Robin looked at them, she took a deep breath and prayed that the meeting would go well. Sundance was meant for Craig and Zack and Will, and she couldn't allow herself to think where she might fit into the picture. The important thing now was for Craig to get that loan.

Her mind was racing ahead, and she couldn't help wondering if there was something she could do to help.

Then it hit her. She had to talk with Kathy. It was the least she could do! There was still time to reach her before Craig arrived at the bank in Cranbrook.

No, her conscience nagged. She had promised him she would stay out of it, she had promised! Still…if he was turned down again, if Uncle Doug didn't see the potential on paper this time…

She knew what she was going to do, and she couldn't stop herself. She cupped her hand to her lips and yelled down to the guys.

"Harley, I have to run to the grocery. Be back within an hour."

He nodded and waved her off. Dashing into the house, she grabbed her purse and car keys and hurried out the door. She would drive to Caribou Creek, call Kathy, and…what? She would swear Kathy to secrecy. But Uncle Doug simply had to know that Robin was involved in this new plan; maybe it would make a difference. Maybe at last the family connection would do some good.

Craig's meeting with Doug Spencer at the bank went surprisingly well. From the beginning, the man showed far more interest in Craig's plan than he had expected. Spencer was a tall, thin man who wore glasses and looked as though he had spent most of his life puttering in the vaults of the bank, counting all the money.

"So you see, sir," Craig pointed to his outline, "I have more than one way to make money on Sundance. I have twelve good horses now, and I have the capital to buy more. I can offer trail rides and riding lessons, special trips for photographing wildlife. I can even board horses for people in town who have a horse or would like to have one."

"Do you have the accommodations for all this?" he asked politely, stroking his chin. Behind his horn-rimmed glasses, the hazel eyes were keen with interest.

"Yes, but I plan to expand, of course, and I have two good carpenters who can work with me on the project. Also, I want to start using the stream; we could have a catch-and-release program on the fishing.

"In addition to fixing up the original Russell cabin, I'd like to build five more, which would be replicas of the original. We could accommodate guests in a real frontier setting. I plan to have a roundup of the horses every morning, where guests could participate if they liked, and then have a big cowboy breakfast back at the house."

Spencer nodded. "That sounds good to me."

Craig nodded, feeling he was winning the man over. "If you'll check my figures, you'll see that the operating loan I'm requesting is reasonable, and I should be able to pay it back with interest at the end of next year."

Spencer nodded, staring thoughtfully at the plans before him. "I think you've got an excellent plan here. And the merchants in the area will certainly go for it. They're always after us to come up with something that will bring in more tourist trade."

He came to his feet. "Naturally, I'll have to discuss this with the board, but I think you can count on the operating loan from us." He extended his hand. "Good luck on your new venture."

Craig wanted to leap across the desk and hug the man, but he settled for a firm handshake. "Thanks for your help."

As he left Spencer's office, he almost collided with Kathy, who was wearing a big smile today.

"Hi, Craig. How's it going?"

"Wonderful. I have some new plans under way, and your father is very encouraging. I think I'll be able to get an operating loan here."

"Super," Kathy smiled. Her eyes twinkled. "I'll be looking forward to the barbecue."

He nodded, a bit puzzled, then hurried on out to his truck. *What did she mean by that?*

As he started up the truck and drove out of town, he kept wondering about Kathy's remark.

He had suggested a barbecue to Robin if he got the loan. Was it just a coincidence that Kathy had mentioned a barbecue? Specifically, a barbecue! Kathy couldn't know about that unless she had talked to Robin.

Then it hit him, and he slammed his fist against the steering wheel. Robin had talked to Kathy. That was why Spencer had seemed so agreeable; it was probably why he was getting the loan. A family favor, rather than his brilliant ideas and detailed paperwork!

His brows lowered over his eyes as he glared at the road. Robin had promised him she wouldn't interfere. He couldn't believe she had broken that promise. If so, could he really trust her? About anything? His mind struggled between defending her and accepting the truth. It was so important to do things on his own. If she interfered on this, what would she do in the future? He slumped back into the seat, brooding over it.

Maybe he was jumping to conclusions. But there was one way to find out for sure.

Robin was working on a chicken stew when Craig walked into the kitchen.

"Well?" Her eyes searched his face, looking for a clue to how the morning went.

"You called Kathy," he said, looking across at her. "I know you did."

She struggled to keep her eyes level with his, but already she could feel herself caving in. She couldn't lie to him.

"Why do you say that?" She could hear the slight tremor in her voice, and she was beginning to dislike what was going on.

He frowned at her, wishing she had denied it. "Because Uncle Doug," he drawled, "practically met me with open arms. And Kathy mentioned our little barbecue celebration."

Robin stared at him for a moment, wishing she could dredge up some excuse, but she couldn't. Nor could she deceive him.

She sat down hard in the chair and stared at the floor. "I just asked her to see that you got a fair chance, that's all."

"Well, I got more than a fair chance. I got some family backing! Why couldn't you stay out of it, Robin? You know I needed to do this on my own."

She leaped out of the chair and began to pace the opposite side of the room. "Why are you unwilling to accept any help I want to give?"

"The help you want to give is to invest your life's savings and then press your relatives to bail me out." His voice was low and controlled, too controlled, Robin thought. His face was a cold hard mask; his lips a straight line.

"I didn't press my relatives to do anything. You and your plan sold my uncle, not my part in it. But I don't think it's my relatives that we're really talking about; I think it's an overdose of pride on your part." She glared at him. "That's your problem, you know. You won't let anyone help you. Things have to be done your way."

"My way? You and your cousin deceived me from the very beginning. You're just dying to stake a claim on this land, and you seem to be doing a good job of trying to stake a claim on me and my sons."

Robin's head snapped back. His words scalded her with humiliation, and she fought the ache in her throat and the temptation to burst into tears. Instead, she turned and walked out of the kitchen, her head high.

Once she reached the guest bedroom and closed the door, she snatched open the drawers and began to pack her clothes. No words had ever hurt her more, and the tears she fought to control rushed hotly to her eyes and trickled down her cheeks.

She heard a back door slam and boots thud over the porch as Craig made his way down to the barn.

Good. She wouldn't have to look at him again or fight with him anymore. She could leave quietly with no further words to him. Trying not to sob or feel the awful pain in her heart, she packed the last pair of jeans into her duffel bag. Then she reached for her guitar.

Her tears formed a dark spot on the guitar case, and she fumbled around the room, searching for a Kleenex. Finding one, she sat down on the side of the bed and allowed herself one good hard cry. It was all that would cleanse her soul, that and maybe a prayer or two.

But she didn't feel like praying. Her eyes strayed to Jenny Russell's Bible on the nightstand. She took a deep shaky breath and reached for it. It would help if she would read the verse on the inside of the cover, but she hadn't the heart for it. Maybe someday back in Calgary, she could sort it all out. But it was going to take a long time for this hurt to heal, if it ever did.

Carefully, she packed the Bible in her duffel bag and looked around the room one last time. Through the window, she could see Craig mounting Chief. Turning the big horse's head, he dug in his heels, and the two became a dark red streak across the meadow.

Harley walked out of the barn, staring after him. He turned his head toward the house then, removed his hat, and scratched his head, obviously puzzled.

She couldn't imagine what he had said to them; probably nothing. He had probably just gone in with that surly frown that he wore when things didn't go his way. Maybe he snapped at the boys and Harley, or maybe he was too angry to speak to anyone.

Then, a white head darted around a corner of the barn, and Zack was bounding up the path to the house. Will came out of the barn, running up the path behind Zack. They were probably coming to the house, expecting lunch, half starved. How was she going to tell them good-bye? It would be the hardest part of leaving Sundance. That and forgetting Craig. But she couldn't think about that part of it now. She had to face the boys; she had to find the right words to say good-bye.

Twenty-Nine

❧

W hat do you mean you have to go home?" Zack stormed at her. "You can't leave."

"Yes, she can, Zack," Will said, looking pale and angry. "We don't need her here. We never did. All she does is upset Dad."

Robin stared at Will, unable to believe such harsh criticism coming from the little boy who had seemed so kind, so gentle.

She swallowed hard, feeling the deep wave of hurt rising again. "Will," she said kindly, "I'm sorry you feel that way. I want you guys to know," she looked from Will to Zack, "that I would like to be your friend. Always."

"How can we be friends if you go off?" Zack demanded, quite logically.

She sighed. "Maybe you could come to Calgary to see me. Hey, you could come over for the Stampede."

They exchanged shocked glances, then the hopeful expression on Will's face turned grim again. "We can't go, Zack. If Dad's mad at her, he won't let us go."

"Listen to me." She leaned over, forcing Will to look her squarely in the eye. "I don't want you guys disappointed just because we grownups can't settle our differences. If you can't come to the Stampede this year, maybe next year or the next. Anyway, I've enjoyed spending some time with you guys. I think you're really terrific."

Tears filled her eyes and trickled down her cheeks.

Zack's blue eyes widened, and he froze in his tracks, staring at her, obviously unsure what to say or do. Will, in contrast, yanked free of her hand, stormed out of the kitchen, and headed for his room.

"I hate you," he called over his shoulder. "I don't ever want to see you again."

Robin closed her eyes, stunned by his words. Then suddenly she felt a rough little hand in hers, and she opened her eyes and looked at Zack. The blue eyes that had so often danced with mischief now looked at her with a sweetness that brought more tears to her eyes.

"He doesn't mean that. And neither does Dad."

She swallowed hard, reaching for a napkin to dry her face. "Thanks, Zack. You're the only one who seems to understand."

Turning, she reached for her suitcase. Zack already had a grasp on the guitar and was lugging it to the door for her. Neither of them spoke as she walked to the Toyota, wishing she could say good-bye to Harley and Sam. But she had already said too many good-byes. The ache in her heart was a physical pain.

She turned her eyes briefly toward the far end of the valley, thinking about the log cabin and the dreams she had for it. Then she squared her shoulders and took a deep breath. She forced herself to walk toward the car, toward the little boy waiting in front of her, trying so hard to be the gentleman of the family.

She opened the trunk and put in her duffel bag, then her guitar case. As she slammed the trunk, she looked down at

Zack, whose eyes were suspiciously moist.

"Nobody hugged me good-bye," she said.

His little arms flew around her, squeezing hard, amazing her with their strength.

"Thanks, Zack," she said, stroking his blond hair. He smelled of the barnyard and horses and boyish sweat, but it was a smell she would forever treasure.

He released her quickly and bounded toward the house, his blond hair flying, his little boots making fast tracks across the grass Suddenly the sight of Zack, the house, and the land blurred before her, and she got in the Toyota and slammed the door.

"Good-bye, Sundance," she said, cranking the engine.

She dared not look back as she drove away.

Thirty

Craig sat under the cottonwood tree in front of Skook's cabin, deep in thought. Flipping gravel into the stream, he stared at the cabin, recalling how much the place meant to Robin. He believed she wanted to hang onto Sundance as much as he did. The problem was that he had to be his own man. He hadn't made it as a cattle rancher, and he hadn't been smart enough to come up with an alternate plan, as she had so wisely done.

He leaned back on his elbow, closed his eyes, and basked in the cooling breeze drifting through the cottonwoods. The hard ride had chased away the remnants of his anger, and now regret was beginning to set in. No matter what she had done, he shouldn't have yelled at her or behaved the way he did. The truth was, his pride had taken a beating, and he knew that now.

But couldn't she understand how important it was to him to accomplish this on his own? To be his own man? More than that, he needed the objective opinion of a reputable business-man to tell him if his plan looked sound. He wanted the absolute truth if he was going to invest his life here.

He opened his eyes and stared up at the sky. He was thinking about Doug Spencer, a man who would not be swayed unless every i was dotted, every t was crossed. He needed an unbiased opinion from this cool, unflappable man.

He squinted at the sky, watching a raven circle. Could the man be easily biased? If he was so cool and unflappable, would Robin's plea for help really sway him into making a huge loan?

A thoughtful frown settled between his dark brows. No, it wouldn't. Even if Robin had asked him for a loan on Sundance herself, he might have said no without a sound plan. After all, it wasn't his money he was handing out. And there was that board of directors he kept mentioning.

He sat up straighter. In all likelihood, Robin and Kathy had little to do with the man's decision to approve this loan to him. Otherwise, how could he justify it to his board of directors?

Craig's heart began to soften as he thought of Robin, and this time the thoughts were not tinged with anger. So what if she had broken her promise? Was it such a bad thing after all? And even if it was, he couldn't deny one important truth: he was in love with her. The boys loved her, and she had obviously been very good for all of them.

So why had he let his pride make a fool of him?

Pulling himself to his feet, he began to walk toward Chief, who was chomping happily on the thick meadow grass. Recalling the look in her eyes when he had kissed her, he believed she might feel the same for him.

"Well, fella, let's tuck our tail and go say we're sorry," he said, planting his boot into the stirrup. In the saddle, he suddenly felt much better about everything, now that he had resolved the matter in his mind.

Glancing toward the cabin, he thought of Skook and Jenny Russell and some of the things Robin had told him about them.

What was that Bible verse Robin was always quoting that Jenny loved? Something about God being a shield, giving honor and glory. Not withholding anything good from people who tried to…what was it? Walk blamelessly.

As he trotted his horse back down the path, he recalled how he had stood in the yard, gazing up at the sky a few nights ago, asking God to help him hold on to Sundance. And he had promised to walk blamelessly if only God would hear his plea.

He felt an uneasy stirring of his conscience. At last a way had been provided, and for the first time he had real hope. In fact, he could get really excited about Sundance as a guest ranch, rather than a cattle ranch, or even just a horse ranch.

So God had answered his prayer. Then what had Craig done in return? He had lost his temper, said cruel things to Robin, stomped out of the house like a kid. That could hardly be called blameless in anyone's eyes, not even a kind and forgiving God.

He squeezed his legs against the sorrel. The big horse leaped forward, and soon they were burning the wind. All Craig could think about now was getting back to Robin, telling her how sorry he was for the things he had said to her. He wanted to move on with their lives. There was a lot to plan for, hope for. He felt a new kind of joy soaring through him as he and Chief raced home.

Harley met him at the barn, looking both anxious and sheepish. "She's pulled stakes and gone," he yelled to Craig before he was even out of the saddle.

"What?" Craig squinted down at him.

"Robin. She's packed up and gone. Told the boys good-bye."

Craig's head swiveled toward the house, and he could see that Harley was telling the truth. Her car was gone, and the boys were huddled quietly on the front porch. There was no argument in progress; in fact, nothing was going on. And that was indeed a bad sign. Shaking his head, he came off the horse and wordlessly shoved the reins into Harley's hand.

He hurried up the path to the front porch where his sons sat, grim and silent.

"How long has she been gone?" he called. Zack had already jumped up to deliver the news, but that question stumped him for a few seconds.

"Uh…" Zack looked uncertainly at Will.

"What difference does it make?" Will grumbled. "She doesn't care about us. She's gone home."

Craig stopped at the foot of the porch steps, taking note of Will's red eyes and the bitter tone of voice. His eyes shot to Zack, who had turned around to glare at Will. Zack took a step toward his brother, his fists balled.

"She did too care," Zack argued. "If it hadn't been for her, you wouldn't know anything about your arrowhead collection."

"And you wouldn't be such a brat," Will lashed back. "Everybody pets you. She liked you best."

"No, she didn't," Zack shouted, squaring off, ready for a good fight to clear the air.

Will jumped up, needing a good one himself.

"Hold it," Craig said, taking the steps two at a time. He stepped between the two little boys who were again hiding their feelings behind their anger. "Now let's just have a little talk here. I want to know how you boys feel about Robin."

Will glared at Zack another few seconds before he turned to face his father.

"It's how you feel that counts," Will snapped. "You're the one who got her so upset. If not for you, she wouldn't have left."

Craig nodded. "You're right, Will. I'm the reason she left."

"She didn't want to go," Zack said, the anger fading from his face. "She was crying…"

Will and his father exchanged troubled glances, and for a moment nobody spoke.

"Well," Craig removed his baseball cap and ran a hand over his hair, damp from the heat and the trauma. "I'll tell you how I feel."

The sight of two little upturned faces, eyes filled with trust, wrenched at his heart. Couldn't he ever learn?

"Robin brought a lot of good into our lives," he said. "She really cared about you boys, and not just because you were my sons or because you lived here at the ranch. She liked each of you for the special people that you are."

"Does she care about you?" Will asked quietly.

Craig sighed. "I think she does, or she did, if only I had given her a chance."

There was a moment of thoughtful silence. Then Zack came up with a simple, yet obvious, solution.

"Then why don't you give her a chance, Dad?"

"Yes, why don't I?"

Craig slapped his cap on his head and glanced at the pick-up, wondering if Harley had left the gas tank on empty. "I was wrong, and I'm sorry. And I'm going to be man enough to tell her so."

After a quick change of clothes, all three were in the pickup, roaring down the driveway. Zack and Will wore their new cowboy hats; Craig had misplaced his.

"Dad, we gonna chase her all the way to Alberta?" Zack yelled. His small hand gripped the dashboard, his knuckles white.

Craig glanced at Zack, hunkered down in the middle of the cab. For the first time all day, he noticed the sweat rings on Zack's neck. "Zack, why didn't you wash up?" He reached over, trying to wipe beads of dirt from Zack's neck.

"Dad, you're gonna break my neck!" Zack protested.

"If he doesn't kill us first!" Will yelled as they hit the cattle guard and almost went airborne.

Craig grabbed a breath, making a conscious effort to slow down as he skidded onto Sundance Road leading back to the highway.

Robin tried to get a grip on her emotions as she drove along, wiping her face with a Kleenex.

Don't think about it now, she told herself. *Deal with it later; otherwise, you'll be off in the ditch again.* But the memory of the ditch only brought a painful reminder of meeting Craig for the first time.

She made a conscious effort to slow down, although she was practically creeping now. She felt as though she had left her heart in the yard at Sundance, that the rest of her had gone on remote, moving along as stiffly as a robot, obeying commands from a voice of logic that had taken over in her head.

Well, she'd get back to Calgary and make yet another new start. How many times in her life was she going to do that?

Taking a deep breath, she pressed her lips together. No, she mustn't think about that either. She would make as many new starts as it took to settle this restlessness in her soul.

But you settled it back there at Sundance, her conscience nagged. *Why did you have to lose your temper? Why did you have to get so stubborn?*

"Because there is a limit to how much manure I'll take from Craig Cameron," she said aloud.

Suddenly, she was starving. Not for an apple or some carrot sticks, but for something sinful and gooey. Like a chocolate bar with plenty of nuts. And a Coke. She could drink three Cokes in a gulp. Chips. Chips would be good. Salty and crusty. She could load up on snacks and munch her way back to Calgary!

Nearing the main highway, Craig had to make a decision. Did Robin turn north to go over Kicking Horse Pass into Banff and on to Calgary, or did she turn south? Turning south would take her to Fort Steele where she could turn and go over Crows Nest Pass and back up to Calgary.

He decided to head south toward Fort Steele. He recalled she had mentioned coming over Crows Nest Pass when she came from Alberta.

Craig was driving faster with each mile, wondering all the while if he had chosen the right highway for catching up with her. She hadn't had time to get far; he should have caught up by now, unless she, too, was burning up the road.

Robin turned in at the Quick and Easy, spotting the pay phone at the end of the building. Her first inclination had been to head to Cranbrook, storm into the bank, and give Kathy a piece of her mind for telling Craig…whatever she told him. Then, she had changed her mind. A simple phone call would do. Thank you very much for ruining my life, cousin.

She could think of a dozen different openers, and she hoped the phone call would upset her blabbermouth cousin—third cousin, however many times removed. In fact, she hoped Kathy would be so disturbed that she would be unable to count out money at the teller window. Better yet, she hoped she'd be messing up for the next five years. She deserved it for not keeping her mouth shut.

Robin glanced at her fuel gauge. The needle pointed dangerously to empty, and she realized with a sinking heart that she could easily have run out of gas before she'd ever thought about it.

Pulling up to the gas tanks, she cut the engine.

Thirty - One

No one spoke as Craig barreled past other vehicles, with Zack and Will peering in every direction. Once they reached Fort Steele and the road leading to Cranbrook, he slowed down. Did she go to Cranbrook to say good-bye to her cousin, or did she turn east for Crows Nest Pass?

"Dad, the light changed," Will prompted.

"I'm trying to decide which way to go. I'll think we'll take a chance she went to Cranbrook."

"What if she didn't?" Will worried.

"If she didn't, Will, we'll go to Calgary and see the Stampede," Zack patiently explained.

"Son, the Stampede is a couple weeks away," Craig growled, darting glances toward parking lots along the way. "No, we're going to believe that she went to Cranbrook."

Robin finished filling her tank, then got back in the car to move it. Grabbing some of the quarters that she kept in her ashtray, she plunged into her purse for the tiny notebook of addresses and telephone numbers. Finding it, she hopped out of the car and headed for the telephone. She was going to tell Kathy a thing or two, she thought, as her famous temper started to rise again. *Right after I get some munchies.*

Just as they reached the outskirts of Cranbrook, Will yelled.

"There's her car at the Quick and Easy, Dad."

Craig's head spun around as the big truck plunged past. In that split second, he couldn't be sure it was her car; still, he made a fast U-turn, spun gravel onto the shoulder, skidded back onto the pavement, and roared into the parking lot.

Inside, Robin was paying for her fuel and her assortment of goodies. She tried to smile at the friendly clerk, but her lips just wouldn't move in that direction. She felt a hurt in her soul the size of the Grand Canyon. Since she couldn't smile, she decided to try a bit of conversation.

"I need something to munch on," she said. "And who wants to nibble on carrot sticks?"

"Not me!" replied the plump lady, who was admiring Robin's various selections as she placed them gently into a brown paper bag. "For sure, not me," she said with a wide smile that crinkled her double chin. "Have a good day."

Robin sighed. "Thanks. You, too." She turned and walked out the door of the market.

And froze.

Thirty-Two

❧

T he white truck had parked beside her car, and now Craig, Will, and Zack were walking toward her.

"We've been looking for you," Zack announced proudly.

Her eyes locked with Craig's, and for a moment, nobody said anything.

"Whatcha got in the sack?" Zack asked, tugging at a corner.

The bulging sack ripped beneath his tugging fingers, and chips and candy bars toppled everywhere.

"You said we shouldn't eat that stuff," Zack grinned at her. He was delighted to have caught her messing up.

"Robin, could we talk?" Craig asked, nudging Zack aside and kneeling to collect her spilled items.

Will slipped his hand in hers and looked at her with dark pleading eyes. "I'm sorry. I didn't mean what I said." Tears were gathering in the corners of his eyes, and Robin's heart melted.

"I know you didn't, Will," she said, swallowing hard. She had finally gained some self-control, but she was on the brink of losing it again.

"Robin, could we talk?" Craig said again, staring at her. He was holding an armful of snacks which he seemed to have forgotten as he looked into Robin's face.

Without a word, Will rushed inside to grab another sack for her. "Here, Dad," he said, opening the sack for Craig to deposit all the goodies.

Robin looked from Zack to Will, smiling at first one and then the other. "Thanks, guys. Help yourselves; that is, if your dad doesn't object."

"I don't," he said, never taking his eyes off Robin. "In fact," he finally glanced their way, "why don't you guys excuse us for a minute? Go sit in the truck, maybe."

Armed with goodies, the boys made a dash for the truck while Craig walked Robin to her Toyota. They leaned against the side of the car and looked at one another for several seconds before Craig finally swallowed the last of his pride.

"I am so sorry," he said. "Like Will, I didn't mean what I said to you. I wish I could take those words back, but since I can't, all I can do is apologize from the bottom of my heart."

Robin took a deep breath and tore her eyes from his. "Obviously, I got carried away, too. But the truth is, the ranch belongs to you, and what you do with it is your business. It's hard for me to stay objective; in fact, I can't. So that's why I'm going home."

She tried not to think about the boys over in the truck or the way her heart ached as she stood beside Craig. Instead she made one last desperate attempt to be practical. Someone had to be, she decided, glancing again at Craig. She had never seen him so upset.

"I've enjoyed my visit, but I'm not part of your life."

It took all her strength to say those words, but she knew she must.

"Yes, you are a part of my life." He reached for her hand and gripped it gently. "Robin, you've changed my life completely, and you've helped the boys tremendously."

"Well, if I've helped, I'm glad. But I have a life, too, Craig, and I need to get on with it—"

"The ranch may have been named Sundance by your great-grandparents, but there's been no sun in it for me, no joy at all with you gone. And there won't be if you don't come back."

Slowly, her eyes drifted to his face, climbing around the sensuous curve of his lips, up the broad cheeks, to meet the dark eyes. She could see he was sincere, that he meant those words. And yet, what did he expect of her? What did he want from her? She couldn't go on being on the fringes of their life, standing on the outside looking in.

"So what are you saying?" she managed to ask.

"I'm saying that I'm crazy in love with you. Right now, my heart is beating like a tom-tom. Don't go, Robin. Please give us another chance."

Her mouth dropped open as she looked into his dark eyes and saw the love mirrored there. She released her pent-up breath and slowly lifted her hand to his face and began to stroke his cheek. "I'm in love with you, too," she said, smiling into his eyes. "But I don't know what we're going to do about your pride and my flaring temper."

"Maybe we'll just have to do like Will and Zack, get out on the front porch and have a good shouting match when we feel like it." He put his arm around her pulling her against his chest. "Just don't leave us. Please don't ever leave us again. Let's get married," he said suddenly. "I realize you can't go on living under my roof as you have in the past. You need a commitment from me. I understand that. And—"

"Hold it, cowboy," she laughed. "Let's just slow down and think about this a bit more. On the way back to the ranch."

They were both laughing now, and the tears that Robin had fought to hold back leaped forward and trickled down her cheeks. This time they were tears of joy.

"Then what are we waiting for?" Craig hugged her. "We need to go home and start making plans. That barbecue could turn into a real celebration; in fact, I think it should!"

He leaned down and kissed her passionately. And in the background one small voice called out: "Way to go, Dad!"

Dear Reader,

This story has been very special to me because I spent my first year of married life in British Columbia. Many years have passed since then, but we have returned several times to visit friends throughout Canada who are the most gracious, most wonderful people on earth.

Sundance Ranch and its characters are a composite of many people we have known in Canada, with the exception of Zack and Will, modeled after our sons, Lan and Steve. I had so much fun writing this book because it allowed me to recall many endearing experiences in our family life. The halloween mask was Steve's little joke, and tender-hearted Will, always trying to help, is a young Lan.

God has blessed me so very much with two wonderful sons and a marvelous daughter. I have been equally blessed with a husband and soulmate who has shared life's journeys with me. During his recovery from open-heart surgery, he was a tremendous help in this story. His knowledge of history and geography were essential, along with his feel for frontier life.

Despite two critical illnesses this year—involving my husband and my mother—God gave me the physical and mental energy to complete this story. I know an added blessing was the fun of writing it at a time when I needed some fun in my life.

To those of you who have written, know that you are all very special to me. I never forget that you are the ones who really count when I am thinking of stories and plots.

Peggy Darty

Write to Peggy Darty
c/o Palisades
P.O.Box 1720
Sisters, Oregon 97759

PALISADES...PURE ROMANCE

⌁ PALISADES ⌁

Reunion, Karen Ball
Refuge, Lisa Tawn Bergren
Torchlight, Lisa Tawn Bergren
Treasure, Lisa Tawn Bergren
Chosen, Lisa Tawn Bergren
Firestorm, Lisa Tawn Bergren (October, 1996)
Cherish, Constance Colson
Angel Valley, Peggy Darty
Seascape, Peggy Darty
Sundance, Peggy Darty
Love Song, Sharon Gillenwater
Antiques, Sharon Gillenwater
Secrets, Robin Jones Gunn
Whispers, Robin Jones Gunn
Echoes, Robin Jones Gunn
Coming Home, Barbara Jean Hicks
Glory, Marilyn Kok
Sierra, Shari MacDonald
Forget-Me-Not, Shari MacDonald
Diamonds, Shari MacDonald (November, 1996)
Westward, Amanda MacLean
Stonehaven, Amanda MacLean
Everlasting, Amanda MacLean
Betrayed, Lorena McCourtney
Escape, Lorena McCourtney (September, 1996)
Voyage, Elaine Schulte

A Christmas Joy, Darty, Gillenwater, MacLean
Mistletoe, Ball, Hicks, McCourtney (October, 1996)

THE PALISADES LINE

*Ask for them at your local bookstore. If the title you seek is not in stock,
the store may order you a copy using the ISBN listed.*

Reunion, Karen Ball
ISBN 0-88070-951-0
There are wolves on Taylor Sorensen's ranch. Wildlife biologist Connor
Alexander is sure of it. So he takes a job as a ranch hand to prove it. Soon he
and Taylor are caught in a fierce controversy—and in a determined battle
against the growing attraction between them...an attraction that neither can
ignore.

Chosen, Lisa Tawn Bergren
ISBN 0-88070-768-2
When biblical archeologist Alexsana Rourke is handed the unprecedented
honor of excavating Solomon's Stables in Jerusalem, she has no idea that she'll
need to rely heavily upon the new man in her life—CNN correspondent Ridge
McIntyre—and God, to save her.

Refuge, Lisa Tawn Bergren
ISBN 0-88070-875-1 (New ISBN)
Part One: A Montana rancher and a San Francisco marketing exec—only one
incredible summer and God could bring such diverse lives together. *Part Two:*
Lost and alone, Emily Walker needs and wants a new home, a sense of family.
Can one man lead her to the greatest Father she could ever want and a life full
of love?

Firestorm, Lisa Tawn Bergren (October, 1996)
ISBN 0-88070-953-7
In the sequel to Bergren's best-selling *Refuge, Firestorm* tells the romantic tale
of two unlikely soulmates: a woman who fears fire, and the man who loves it.
Reyne Oldre wasn't always afraid, but a tragic accident one summer changed
her forever. Can Reyne get beyond her fear and give her heart to smoke
jumper Logan McCabe?

Torchlight, Lisa Tawn Bergren
ISBN 0-88070-806-9
When beautiful heiress Julia Rierdon returns to Maine to remodel her family's
estate, she finds herself torn between the man she plans to marry and unexpected feelings for a mysterious wanderer who threatens to steal her heart.

Treasure, Lisa Tawn Bergren
ISBN 0-88070-725-9
She arrived on the Caribbean island of Robert's Foe armed with a lifelong dream—to find her ancestor's sunken ship—and yet the only man who can help her stands stubbornly in her way. Can Christina and Mitch find their way to the ship *and* to each other?

Cherish, Constance Colson
ISBN 0-88070-802-6
Recovering from the heartbreak of a failed engagement, Rose Anson seeks refuge at a resort on Singing Pines Isalnd, where she plans to spend a peaceful summer studying and painting the spectacular scenery of international Lake of the Woods. But when a flamboyant Canadian and a big-hearted American compete for her love, the young artist must face her past—and her future. What follows is a search for the source and meaning of true love: a journey that begins in the heart and concludes in the soul.

Angel Valley, Peggy Darty
ISBN 0-88070-778-X
When teacher Laurel Hollingsworth accepts a summer tutoring position for a wealthy socialite family, she faces an enormous challenge in her young student, Anna Lee Wentworth. However, the real challenge is ahead of her: hanging on to her heart when older brother Matthew Wentworth comes to visit. Soon Laurel and Matthew find that they share a faith in God...and powerful feelings for one another. Can Laurel and Matthew find time to explore their relationship while she helps the emotionally troubled Anna Lee and fights to defend her love for the beautiful *Angel Valley*?

Seascape, Peggy Darty
ISBN 0-88070-927-8
On a pristine sugar sand beach in Florida, Jessica has a lot to reflect upon. The untimely death of her husband, Blake—and the sudden entrance of a new man, distracting her from her grief. In the midst of opening a B&B, can Jessica overcome her anger and forgive the one responsible for Blake's death? Loving the mysterious new man in her life will depend upon it.

Sundance, Peggy Darty
ISBN 0-88070-952-9
Follow Robin Grayson to the wilds of British Columbia, Canada, where she meets Craig Cameron, a widowed rancher with two small sons who desperately need a mother. Is free-spirited Robin ready to settle down in the 1990's last wild frontier?

Love Song, Sharon Gillenwater
ISBN 0-88070-747-X

When famous country singer Andrea Carson returns to her hometown to recuperate from a life-threatening illness, she seeks nothing more than a respite from the demands of stardom that have sapped her creativity and ability to perform. It's Andi's old high school friend, Wade Jamison, who helps her to realize that she needs inner healing as well. As Andi's strength grows, so do her feelings for the rancher who has captured her heart. But can their relationship withstand the demands of her career? Or will their romance be as fleeting as a beautiful *Love Song*?

Antiques, Sharon Gillenwater
ISBN 0-88070-801-8

Deeply wounded by the infidelity of his wife, widower Grant Adams swore off all women—until meeting charming antiques dealer Dawn Carson. Although he is drawn to her, Grant struggles to trust again. Dawn finds herself overwhelmingly attracted to the darkly brooding cowboy, but won't marry a nonbeliever. As Grant learns more about her faith, he is touched by its impact on her life and slowly begins to trust.

Echoes, Robin Jones Gunn
ISBN 0-88070-773-9

In this dramatic romance filled with humor, Lauren Phillips enters the wild, uncharted territory of the Internet on her home computer and "connects" with a man known only as "KC." Recovering from a broken engagement and studying for her teaching credential, her correspondence with KC becomes the thing she enjoys most. Will their e-mail romance become a true love story when they meet face to face?

Secrets, Robin Jones Gunn
ISBN 0-88070-721-6

Seeking a new life as an English teacher in a peaceful Oregon town, Jessica tries desperately to hide the details of her identity from the community...until she falls in love. Will the past keep Jessica and Kyle apart forever?

Whispers, Robin Jones Gunn
ISBN 0-88070-755-0

Teri Moreno went to Maui eager to rekindle a romance. But when circumstances turn out to be quite different than she expects, she finds herself spending a great deal of time with a handsome, old high school crush who now works at a local resort. But the situation becomes more complicated when Teri meets Gordon, a clumsy, endearing Australian with a wild past, and both men begin to pursue her. Will Teri respond to God's gentle urgings toward true love? The answer lies in her response to the gentle *Whispers* in her heart.

Coming Home, Barbara Hicks
ISBN 0-88070-945-6
Keith Castle is running from a family revelation that destroyed his world, and deeply hurt his heart. Katie Brannigan is the childhood friend who was wounded by his sudden disappearance. Together, Keith and Katie could find healing and learn that in his own time, God manages all things for good. But can Katie bring herself to give love one more chance?

Glory, Marilyn Kok
ISBN 0-88070-754-2
To Mariel Forrest, the teaching position in Taiwan provided more than a simple escape from grief; it also offered an opportunity to deal with her feelings toward the God she once loved, but ultimately blamed for the death of her family. Once there, Mariel dares to ask the timeless question: "If God is good, why do we suffer?" What follows is an inspiring story of love, healing, and renewed confidence in God's goodness.

Diamonds, Shari MacDonald (November, 1996)
ISBN 0-88070-982-0
When spirited sportscaster Casey Foster inherits a minor league team, she soon discovers that baseball isn't all fun and games. Soon, Casey is juggling crazy promotional events, major league expectations, and egos of players like Tucker Boyd: a pitcher who wants nothing more than to return to the major leagues—until Casey captures his heart and makes him see diamonds in a whole new way.

Forget-Me-Not, Shari MacDonald
ISBN 0-88070-769-0
Traveling to England's famed Newhaven estate to pursue an internship as a landscape architect, Hayley Buckman looked forward to making her long-held career dreams come true. But upon arrival, Hayley is quickly drawn to the estate and its mysterious inhabitants, despite a sinister warning urging her to leave. Will an endearing stranger help her solve the mystery and find love as well?

Sierra, Shari MacDonald
ISBN 0-88070-726-7
When spirited photographer Celia Randall travels to eastern California for a short-term assignment, she quickly is drawn to—and locks horns with—editor Marcus Stratton. Will lingering heartaches destroy Celia's chance at true love? Or can she find hope and healing high in the *Sierra*?

Westward, Amanda MacLean
ISBN 0-88070-751-8
Running from a desperate fate in the South toward an unknown future in the West, plantation-born artist Juliana St. Clair finds herself torn between two men, one an undercover agent with a heart of gold, the other a man with evil intentions and a smooth facade. Witness Juliana's dangerous travels toward faith and love as she follows God's lead in this powerful historical novel.

Stonehaven, Amanda MacLean
ISBN 0-88070-757-7
Picking up in the years following *Westward, Stonehaven* follows Callie St. Clair back to the South where she has returned to reclaim her ancestral home. As she works to win back the plantation, the beautiful and dauntless Callie turns it into a station on the Underground Railroad. Covering her actions by playing the role of a Southern belle, Callie risks losing Hawk, the only man she has ever loved. Readers will find themselves quickly drawn into this fast-paced novel of treachery, intrigue, spiritual discovery, and unexpected love.

Everlasting, Amanda MacLean
ISBN 0-88070-929-4
Picking up where the captivating *Stonehaven* left off, *Everlasting* brings readers face to face once more with charming, courageous—and very Irish—Sheridan O'Brian. Will she find her missing twin? And will Marcus Jade, a reporter bent on finding out what really happened to Shamus, destroy his chances with her by being less than honest?

Betrayed, Lorena McCourtney
ISBN 0-88070-756-9
As part of a wealthy midwestern family, young Rosalyn Fallon was sheltered from the struggles brought on by the Depression. But when her father's company collapses and her boyfriend and best friend elope, Rosalyn unexpectedly finds herself facing both hardship and heartbreak. Will her new life out West and a man as rugged and rough as the land itself help her recover?

Escape, Lorena McCourtney (September, 1996)
ISBN 1-57673-012-3
Is money really everything? The winsome Beth Curtis must come to terms with that question as she fights to hold on to guardianship of her nephew, even facing her deceased sister-in-law's brother. Sent to collect the boy, handsome Guy Wilkerson has no idea that he will fall for Beth, and come to see his own family's ways of living in a new light. Can the two overcome such diversity to be together, beginning their own family?

Voyage, Elaine Schulte
ISBN 1-57673-011-5
Traveling via ship to the Holy Land, Ann Marie is on a pilgrimage, discovering things about faith and love all the way. But will a charming man who guides her—among the romantic streets of Greece and elsewhere—distract her from the One who truly loves her?

A Christmas Joy, MacLean, Darty, Gillenwater
ISBN 0-88070-780-1 (same length as other Palisades books)
Snow falls, hearts change, and love prevails! In this compilation, three experienced Palisades authors spin three separate novelettes centering around the Christmas season and message.
By Amanda MacLean: A Christmas pageant coordinator in a remote mountain village of Northern California is reunited with an old friend and discovers the greatest gift of all.
By Peggy Darty: A college ski club reunion brings together model Heather Grant and an old flame. Will they gain a new understanding?
By Sharon Gillenwater: A chance meeting in an airport that neither of them could forget—and a Christmas reunion.

Mistletoe: Ball, Hicks, McCourtney (October, 1996)
ISBN 1-57673-013-1
A new Christmas anthology of three novellas...all in one keepsake book!

Also look for our new line:
PALISADES PREMIER
More Story. More Romance.

Chase the Dream, Constance Colson
ISBN 0-88070-928-6, $11.99
Alison Austin's childhood dream of being a world-champion barrel racer leads to problems at home and in the arena. Rising rodeo star Forrest Jackson, wounded from the death of his father and abandonment of his mother, is Alison's ideal—and her cousin Jenny's boyfriend. Ultimately, Alison must decide how much she is willing to give up...and to take.

Raised on the circuit, Jenny's love for Forrest is mixed with her love for barrel racing, while bull rider Tom Rawlings rodeos with much different motives.

As the time runs down and the competition heightens, the destinies of these four entwine, leading to a breathless climax. It's rodeo: the rough-and-tumble sport propelled by dreams; where love, life, and death are separated by mere seconds; and where meeting the Master Rider is inevitable.

Promise Me the Dawn, **Amanda MacLean (September, 1996)**
ISBN 0-88070-955-3, $11.99

Set in turn-of-the-century San Francisco and Monterey, *Promise Me the Dawn* weaves the tender love story of spirited English beauty Molly Quinn and Zachary MacAlister, an immigrant who came to America to flee his family's titles, wealth, and influence. During the dark days that follow the 1906 earthquake, Molly and Zachary plan a future rendezvous in the Pacific cliffs.

After they separate, Molly makes a name for herself and becomes the glamorous, new toast of the town. When Zach proposes, Molly decides that she hasn't lived enough yet, and lets him go. But when she later realizes that she may have lost him for good, Molly must reexamine the desires of her heart and turn back to her God before rediscovering the love she nearly lost in *Promise Me the Dawn.*

AND ESPECIALLY FOR YOUNG ADULTS:
Announcing the exciting new
Pacific Cascades University Series!

Come and meet nine college students and witness their trials and tribulations as they discover more about relationships, college life, and their world.

Freshman Blues, Wendy Lee Nentwig, ISBN 0-88070-947-2
Homeward Heart, Lissa Halls Johnson, ISBN 0-88070-948-0
True Identity, Bernie Sheahan, ISBN 0-88070-949-9 (September 1996)
Spring Break, Wendy Lee Nentwig, ISBN 0-88070-950-2 (September 1996)

If you enjoyed reading *Sundance,* the following is an excerpt from Peggy Darty's novel, *Angel Valley.*

One

⌘

Laurel Hollingsworth, don't say I didn't warn you!"

Ted Fisher, principal of Angel Valley Junior High, looked across his desk at the slim blond woman. Shoulder-length hair styled in a smooth cut framed her oval face and delicate features.

"All right, you've warned me, Ted. But we're only talking about a summer job. Besides, I dealt with difficult children in Atlanta during my first year of teaching." Laurel smiled at the small graying man, thinking how protective he was of his teachers and students.

"And you couldn't wait to get back to the Smoky Mountains!" he teased.

"You're right! And lucky for me, your seventh-grade teacher had decided to retire."

"Lucky for us, you mean! You're one of the best teachers we've ever had. That's why you won Teacher of the Year."

"I bribed the judges," she quipped.

"Nonsense. You have a special way with children." Ted was

well aware of how Laurel threw herself into her work, giving every ounce of energy and knowledge to the students she taught. "Have I ever told you what Matilda Bennett, whom we all know is critical, said about you?"

Laurel lifted an eyebrow. "Maybe you'd better keep it to yourself."

"She said, 'Laurel Hollingsworth can light up a room with her sparkling eyes and warm smile.' She also said you're the darling of Angel Valley."

Laurel stared at Ted, then shook her head. "That's very sweet, but Mrs. Bennett wasn't around when I spoke my mind at the teachers' meeting."

"You were simply refusing to compromise your convictions. There's nothing wrong with that."

"Ted," she said gently, "you seem to be tiptoeing around something. What is it?"

"I'm wondering if I should be recommending you to this haughty-sounding socialite from Atlanta and her emotionally troubled daughter. When she called to inquire about a tutor, she told me that her daughter, Anna Lee, had gone into a depression after her father's death. Now she's fallen behind in her studies and needs to be brought up to eighth-grade level before the next school term. I know you could do it, but do you want to spend your summer that way?"

Laurel nodded thoughtfully. "Are the Wentworths the people who built that mansion out on Raven Ridge?"

Ted grinned. "Their summer place! Incidentally, I met Anna Lee's older brother in the mayor's office when I went to discuss this year's Christmas in the Park. He seems like a nice guy."

"What was he doing in the mayor's office?" Laurel was curious.

"Asking questions about the area. He owns an investment firm in Atlanta. Maybe he's planning to put a business up here."

"I hope not! The last thing we need is an Atlanta businessman trying to change our little community when we're happy just the way we are."

Ted wasn't listening. "If he has money to invest, I should solicit for our Christmas in the Park."

"Good idea. Oh! What time is my appointment?"

Ted glanced at his watch. "Ten o'clock, and I mustn't detain you. Laurel, please don't feel compelled to take this job if you don't want it."

"Thanks, Ted. I'll let you know." Laurel stood and smiled again. Then she headed out the side door of the brick school building. She already knew what her decision would be. Until hearing about this job, the summer had stretched uneventfully before her. She had no plans for a vacation this year; she was saving every dollar for a trip to Europe next summer. She couldn't wait to tour England and France, collecting little treasures from the people and their way of life. She already had plans to display those treasures on a shelf in her classroom and use them as occasional teaching tools.

Crossing the parking lot, she glanced at the sky. Sun rays were being swallowed by gray clouds. She hoped that wasn't a bad omen about her interview with the Wentworths.

Laurel's mind raced on to Anna Lee Wentworth as she hopped into her red compact car and cranked the engine. Laurel understood the pain of losing a father at an early age. It had happened to her. She had been devastated by grief until her Sunday school teacher had given her some special Bible verses. She had memorized those verses, reciting them to herself whenever the dark moments came. And slowly she began to heal.

Laurel drove from the parking lot onto the main street of Angel Valley, Tennessee and glanced up at the Smoky Mountains layered against the horizon. Early morning mist shrouded the peaks in a blue haze, reminding Laurel of the Cherokee words for their mountains: place of blue smoke. All of her life she had loved them, gaining strength and peace simply by gazing at them.

Main Street stretched lazily before her, a neat arrangement of frame and concrete buildings that defied time and weather. Folks breathed a sigh of relief when a four-lane highway was put through over in Newton, steering traffic away from Angel Valley. While neighboring towns like Gatlinburg and Pigeon Forge were bursting with progress, Angel Valley fought against change, holding tight to history and tradition. Several small businesses served the community well—a hardware store, dress shop, post office, drug store, two service stations, and two groceries. The school sat on one end of town, the church and cemetery on the other.

Laurel decided to make a quick stop at the post office to check her mail, hoping for a letter from her mother and Hal. She wheeled into a parking space beside the post office and cut her engine. As she hopped out, a gleaming black Jeep parked two spaces down caught her eye. Someday she hoped to have a vehicle like that one, which was far more suitable for traveling up to Knoxville or over to Asheville during the winter months.

She glanced at her watch, suddenly aware she was going to be late for her appointment if she didn't hurry. Her steps quickened on the pavement as she pushed through the front door with a force that sent her smack into the broad chest of a tall man dressed in Levis and a red polo.

"Ooops, sorry." The deep voice above her belonged to a very handsome man; in fact, Laurel found herself temporarily tongue-tied as she looked up at him, the definition of tall, dark, and handsome. He was over six feet tall, with long legs and broad shoulders. Thick, dark hair framed a square face with nice features, deep blue eyes, and a smile that had paralyzed her.

"Excuse me." His smile widened as he gently sidestepped her and pushed through the door.

Laurel took a deep breath and turned to the postmistress. "Millie, who was that?"

The thin, gray-haired woman peered at Laurel over her glasses as she sorted through a stack of mail. "Don't know. He just breezed in and dropped a letter in the slot. Want me to check it out?"

"No, I'm in a hurry. Just keep an eye out." *As though she wouldn't!* Laurel thought. "Did I get a letter from Mom?"

"Laurel, you know this is the first real vacation they've had! Since they're spending the summer in New England, you can't expect Thelma to write every day."

"Mil-lie!"

"Nothing since the postcard from Boston."

Millie felt it was her duty to be mother hen to everyone in Angel Valley. This included reading over the postcards she sorted. She was, however, a kind and generous woman, the first to arrive on the doorstep with food whenever there was an illness or death. And her peanut brittle was legendary.

Laurel waved to Millie and dashed out the door, searching for the handsome stranger. He was nowhere in sight. Just her luck. She did notice, as she jumped back in her car, that the Jeep was gone. The man and his Jeep were definitely worth pursuing! A romantic notion stirred for the first time since Ryan Thompson had put a bruise on her heart.

She backed out into the street and headed toward Raven

Ridge. A light mist was starting to fall, prompting Laurel to turn on her windshield wipers. Fumbling through her purse, she retrieved the eyeglasses prescribed for driving. Hating the feel of frames on her face, she abandoned glasses most of the time, but today, wanting to do all the right things, she clamped them on. As the turnoff to Raven Ridge loomed ahead, she applied the brake, slowing to make a left turn.

The road snaked up the side of the mountain, and her little car sputtered a protest as she pressed the accelerator.

"Behave," she scolded, peering right to left, eager to see the house that had caused so much speculation.

Several impressive homes had been built in the area after outsiders discovered its cool air and tranquil lifestyle, but the Wentworth mansion was reported to outdo all of them.

Although she was almost five feet six inches, Laurel kept stretching her neck to see over the hood of her car. The road was steep and narrow, switching right to left, climbing past a woods of tall pines. She topped the last hill and there it was: a magnificent, two-story, stone-and-glass structure that seemed to perch on the very top of the world.

Parking beside a black Mercedes, she reached for her purse. She had never been shy, but Ted's warning and the imposing mansion had brought on the same apprehension as a trip to the dentist.

The job will last only a couple of months, she reminded herself, thinking of the money she could tuck away in her savings. Visions of Big Ben and the Eiffel Tower danced in her head, and she took a deep breath and peered into the back seat for her umbrella. Naturally, this was the day she had left it at home.

Sighing, she hopped out of the car and gave the door a push. It's sharp corner caught her leg and she winced and bit her lip.

She wasn't hurt, but now a one-inch run in her hose zipped from her ankle to her knee. *What else could go wrong?* she wondered as she made a dash up the stone walkway to the shelter of a small porch.

Her eyes flew over her navy dress, grateful she was not drenched, as she lifted the brass knocker then jumped when it made a loud BANG.

Tucking her purse under her arm, she surveyed the landscape while waiting for someone to answer the door. The valley—complete with a church steeple and farm houses—resembled Rockwell miniatures at Christmas time.

The door swung open and Laurel faced a tall, thin woman wearing a gray linen pants suit. The woman looked to be in her upper forties or early fifties, judging from the wrinkles bracketing her eyes and mouth. Her brown hair was worn short and straight, whisked back on the sides of her thin face. The russet blush on her sunken cheeks had been applied with a heavy hand, along with the brick-colored lipstick, which merely accented the thinness of her lips. Her eyes were a cold, biting blue.

"Good morning, I'm Laurel Hollingsworth. I'm here to speak with Mrs. Wentworth about a—"

"Come in!"

The woman's abrasive manner shocked Laurel as she crossed the threshold into a slate-tiled foyer.

"This way," the woman called over her shoulder, as she set off down the hall.

Glancing at oil paintings on the walls, Laurel hurried to keep up, following the woman into a huge room where crystal-globed lights danced and twinkled. It was the most gorgeous room Laurel had ever seen.

The house had been created as an extension of the mountains, with entire walls of tinted glass. Between the glass walls, cream-colored panels reached to cathedral ceilings supported by massive beams. At the far end, a huge fireplace held copper and brass. Beside it sat a large, well-stocked woodbox. A sprawling, over-stuffed sofa was flanked by chairs and ottomans upholstered in the same cream, coral, and green as the sofa.

Lush plants filled every corner, along with potted trees, and there were several crystal vases filled with fresh flowers. Richly colored Oriental rugs added warmth to the hardwood floor gleaming at Laurel's feet.

"I'm Madeline Wentworth," the woman said abruptly, turning to Laurel and motioning her to a chair.

"It's nice to meet you," Laurel said, taking a seat.

"Did you bring a résumé?" Madeline asked. Her pale blue eyes swept Laurel up and down.

Laurel bit her lip, wondering why she had overlooked something so important.

"No, I didn't. Mr. Fisher contacted me as I was about to leave town and I came right over."

Madeline looked thoughtful as she lit a cigarette. Laurel watched the woman's jaws sink into deep hollows as she inhaled the smoke.

Laurel cleared her throat, trying not to cough. "I graduated from Lee College with honors," Laurel said. "Then I taught a year in Marietta. The principal's name—"

"Never mind," Madeline waved a jeweled hand. "If you are as capable as your principal says, I don't need a résumé. The important thing is for you to help Anna Lee."

"Well, I believe—"

"Talking about me again, Mother?" A thin insolent voice spoke up.

Laurel turned in her seat and glanced over her shoulder.

Anna Lee Wentworth was short, and Laurel judged her to be at least thirty pounds overweight. Her hair was a dull brown, styled in a short straight bob; her eyebrows were badly in need of tweezers. With all their money, Laurel wondered why the girl had never had a lesson in makeup. At least her skin was smooth, without the acne typical in many girls her age.

Laurel could see little resemblance between mother and daughter, except for the blue eyes. Mrs. Wentworth was almost anorexic, which gave her features a pinched look, while Anna Lee was round in body and face, with full lips thrust into a sullen pout.

The buttons on her embroidered denim shirt were about to pop from the strain of holding cloth together, while the designer jeans were at least two sizes too small. Laurel felt sad just looking at the girl, who had a habit of tugging the front of her shirt lower over her waistline, which Laurel suspected was unbuttoned to accommodate her bulging weight.

"Hello, dear." Madeline got up from the sofa and crossed the room to her daughter's side. "Come meet your new tutor." She placed a hand on her daughter's shoulder.

Anna Lee shrugged her mother's hand away with a disgusted sigh and sauntered into the room.

Laurel stood. "Hi. My name is Laurel Hollingsworth."

Anna Lee glared at her, making no response.

"Anna Lee!" her mother prompted under her breath.

Anna Lee's gaze crawled down Laurel's navy dress and widened on her right leg. Then a smirk curled her lips. Laurel glanced down at the run in her hose, then back at Anna Lee and Madeline, who was now staring at the run, too.

"I don't normally run around with torn hose," Laurel said lightly, trying to make a joke of the incident. "The car door caught me as I was getting out."

Madeline and Anna Lee merely stared at her, not amused. Laurel took a deep breath and mentally counted to ten. *So much for this interview,* she decided, preparing to leave, when Anna Lee suddenly made an outburst, startling her mother as well as Laurel.

"I don't want a tutor!" She glared at her mother. "I told you before we left Atlanta, I can't concentrate. It's no use!"

Laurel heard the desperation in Anna Lee's voice and suddenly saw her as a frustrated girl hiding behind a fácade of anger. Laurel's mind slipped back over the years to that miserable time in her life when she had lost her father at fourteen. She, too, had been overcome with emotions that were difficult to handle. Remembering that trying period, her heart softened as she looked at this pitiful girl who seemed to be trapped in a world of anger and bitterness.

I'll try one more time, Laurel decided.

"I think it would be easier for you to concentrate if you enjoyed your studies. I take field trips with my students and we do lots of projects that really are fun."

Anna Lee and Madeline stared at Laurel as though she were speaking in a foreign language.

"We would take a field trip along the parkway to study the different plants and flowers, and compare them to those in your science book. As for history, I ordered some special books that my students thought were pretty neat."

Laurel read the doubt on Anna Lee's face. Yet, for the first time, there was a different look in her eyes. Laurel hesitated for a moment, glancing from Anna Lee to Madeline Wentworth. "At this time of year it would be a shame not to make the most of being outdoors. I think we could do some hiking, as well."

A spark lit Madeline's dull blue eyes. "A hike? Anna Lee never exercises, so a hike sounds good, don't you think?" She turned to her sulking daughter.

"I don't feel like hiking," Anna Lee snapped.

Laurel took a deep breath. "Well, it's up to you. Perhaps you might want to try another tutor, Mrs. Wentworth." She reached for her purse.

"Okay!" Anna Lee cried. "You can be my tutor. I don't care!"

Heavy steps resounded over the hardwood floor as Anna Lee charged from the room, moving with a speed that surprised Laurel.

Madeline Wentworth stared after the girl, then reached for another cigarette. Her thin face registered weariness and defeat.

"Anna Lee sank into a deep depression after Wilson's death," Madeline said. "She's had a terrible time."

As Laurel looked at the woman's thin face and sunken eyes, it was obvious Madeline had suffered, too.

"Do you want the job?" she asked solemnly.

Laurel considered her options. She faced a tremendous challenge at a time meant for rest and relaxation after a busy school year. With Anna Lee's steps thudding in her ears, Laurel glanced down the hall, wondering why she continued to feel pulled toward this girl. Was she a glutton for punishment?

Suddenly she knew why. Embedded in her mind was the hand-lettered verse, made and framed by a student, resting on her desk at school. The sign seemed to flash before her eyes: *Do unto others as you would have them do unto you.*

Laurel thought of the kind, caring teacher who had gone out of her way to help when Laurel's father died. Now she had been offered a chance to do for someone else what had once been done for her. Long ago Laurel had made a commitment to help troubled children. Here was the perfect opportunity.

She took a deep breath. "Yes, I do."

"Good," Madeline sighed. She walked over to a desk, opened the drawer, and removed a checkbook. "Did Mr. Fisher mention the salary?"

"Yes, he did."

The salary was great, but that was no longer her reason for taking the job. When she saw Madeline reaching for a pen, Laurel spoke up. "Mrs. Wentworth, why don't you wait until I've worked a week before you pay me?"

Madeline eyed her sharply. "I hope that doesn't mean you'll up and quit if you don't like the job. I can't go looking for another tutor; there isn't time."

"If I take the job, I'll keep it," Laurel answered smoothly, trying to ignore Madeline's sharp tone. "I'm just not comfortable with being paid in advance."

Madeline's thin brows arched. "You will be able to begin tomorrow, won't you?" she inquired.

Do I have a choice? Laurel almost asked. "I suppose I can."

"Then we'll count it a full week." She was making a note on the inside of her checkbook.

"That won't be necessary," Laurel responded. "I only expect to be paid for the days I work."

Madeline stared at her, her eyes narrowing for a moment as

though she were suspicious of that answer.

Laurel turned to go. "It was nice meeting you, Mrs. Wentworth."

"Thank you." Despite a brief smile, Madeline's voice was still cold and uncaring.

As Laurel left the house, she was relieved to see the rain had stopped. She got in the car and cranked the engine, glancing again at the house. As her eyes moved up to the second level, she saw Anna Lee standing before a window, staring down at her.

Laurel waved, but Anna Lee merely turned away. Heaving a frustrated sigh, Laurel drove carefully down the winding drive. *This could be the most difficult job I've ever taken,* she decided, as she turned back onto the highway. Still, she felt led to do it. Engrossed in thought as she drove along, she almost missed the black Jeep.

He swept by without looking in her direction, but Laurel caught a glimpse of the handsome stranger she had seen in the post office, the owner of the Jeep. Her eyes shot to her rearview mirror, hurriedly reading the license plate as his turn signal began to flash. Georgia. The Jeep shot from the highway up the road to Raven Ridge.

Who is he? she wondered. *And what business does he have with the Wentworths?*